Cozy Cottage Quilts

In Memory of Bessie Mae Korzilius

LEISURE ARTS, INC.
Little Rock, Arkansas

EDITORIAL STAFF

Vice President and Editor-in-Chief:
Sandra Graham Case
Executive Director of Publications:
Cheryl Nodine Gunnells
Director of Designer Relations: Debra Nettles
Publications Director: Kristine Anderson Mertes
Editorial Director: Susan Frantz Wiles
Photography Director: Lori Ringwood Dimond
Art Operations Director: Jeff Curtis

PRODUCTION
Managing Editor: Cheryl R. Johnson
Senior Technical Writer: Lisa Lancaster

EDITORIAL
Associate Editor: Susan McManus Johnson

ART
Senior Art Director: Rhonda Hodge Shelby
Senior Production Artist: Lora Puls
Production Artists: Ashley Carozza and Dana Vaughn
Color Technician: Mark Hawkins
Photography Stylist: Sondra Daniel and Cassie Newsome
Staff Photographer: Russell Ganser
Publishing Systems Administrator: Becky Riddle
Publishing Systems Assistants: Myra S. Means and
Chris Wertenberger

BUSINESS STAFF

Publisher: Rick Barton
Vice President, Finance: Tom Siebenmorgen
Director of Corporate Planning and Development:
Laticia Mull Cornett
Vice President, Retail Marketing: Bob Humphrey
Vice President, Sales: Ray Shelgosh

Vice President, National Accounts: Pam Stebbins
Director of Sales and Services: Margaret Reinold
Vice President, Operations: Jim Dittrich
Comptroller, Operations: Rob Thieme
Retail Customer Service Manager: Wanda Price
Print Production Manager: Fred F. Pruss

Your home is your haven — let quilts make it cozy! Warm the walls with your own quilted artistry. Make inviting bed quilts and soft, plump pillows. Or piece a quilt for your table. With time-saving techniques like strip piecing, rotary cutting, and machine quilting, your patchwork projects will go together quickly. There's no need to wait any longer to have the serene and pretty "cottage" of your dreams!

Table of Contents

Pastel Posies

The field of delicate blossoms in our Pastel Posies collection will lull a little girl into blissful dreams! The simple flower motif on the pretty quilt, wall hanging, and pillow shams is fused in place and appliquéd with machine stitching.

PASTEL POSIES QUILT

SKILL LEVEL: 1 2 3 4 5
BLOCK SIZE: 8" x 8"
QUILT SIZE: 89" x 97"

YARDAGE REQUIREMENTS

Yardage is based on 45"w fabric.

- [ ] 6 yds of white print
- [ ] $4^1/2$ yds of floral print
- [ ] $3^1/4$ yds of green solid
- [ ] $2^5/8$ yds of pink print
- [ ] $5/8$ yd of light pink solid
  $8^1/8$ yds for backing
  1 yd for binding
  120" x 120" batting

You will also need:
  paper-backed fusible web
  transparent monofilament thread for appliqué

CUTTING OUT THE PIECES

*All measurements include a $1/4$" seam allowance. Follow
Rotary Cutting, page 110, to cut fabric.*

1. **From white print:** ☐
   - Cut 20 **wide strips** $3^1/2$"w.
   - Cut 14 strips 9"w. From these strips, cut
     55 **large squares** 9" x 9".
2. **From floral print:** ☐
   - Cut 10 **narrow strips** $2^1/2$"w.
   - Cut 8 **wide strips** $3^1/2$"w.
   - Cut 2 lengthwise strips $3^1/2$" x 94" for **side
     outer borders**.
   - Cut 2 lengthwise strips $3^1/2$" x 92" for
     top/bottom outer borders.
3. **From green solid:** ☐
   - Cut 2 lengthwise strips $1^1/4$" x 92" for **side
     inner borders**.
   - Cut 2 lengthwise strips $1^1/4$" x 86" for
     top/bottom inner borders.
4. **From pink print:** ☐
   - Cut 19 strips $3^1/2$"w. From these strips, cut
     220 **medium squares** $3^1/2$" x $3^1/2$".
   - Cut 4 **narrow strips** $2^1/2$"w.

PREPARING THE APPLIQUÉS

*Use patterns, page 13, and follow Preparing Appliqué
Pieces, page 116, to cut appliqués.*

1. **From light pink solid:** ☐
   - Cut 55 **Large Circles**.
2. **From pink print:** ☐
   - Cut 55 **Small Circles**.
3. **From green solid:** ☐
   - Cut 55 **Leaves**.
   - Cut 55 **Stems**.

ASSEMBLING THE QUILT TOP

Follow Piecing and Pressing, page 113, to make quilt top.

1. Referring to **Fig. 1**, follow **Invisible Appliqué**, page
   116, to stitch appliqués to centers of **large squares**.
   Trim each **large square** to $8^1/2$" x $8^1/2$".

Fig. 1

2. Place 1 **medium square** on each corner of 1 **large
   square**, right sides together, and stitch diagonally
   as shown in **Fig. 2**. Trim $1/4$" from stitching lines as
   shown in **Fig. 3**. Press open, pressing seam
   allowances toward darker fabric to make **Block A**.
   Make 55 **Block A's**.

Fig. 2   **Fig. 3**

Block A (make 55)

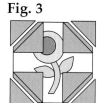

3. Sew 2 **wide strips** and 1 **narrow strip** together to
   make **Strip Set A**. Make 10 **Strip Set A's**. Cut across
   Strip Set A's at $3^1/2$" intervals to make 110 **Unit 1's**.

Strip Set A (make 10)   **Unit 1** (make 110)

$3^1/2$"

4. Sew 2 **wide strips** and 1 **narrow strip** together to
   make **Strip Set B**. Make 4 **Strip Set B's**. Cut across
   Strip Set B's at $2^1/2$" intervals to make 55 **Unit 2's**.

Strip Set B (make 4)   **Unit 2** (make 55)

$2^1/2$"

Sew 2 **Unit 1's** and 1 **Unit 2** together to make **Block B**. Make 55 **Block B's**.

Block B (make 55)

Sew 5 **Block A's** and 5 **Block B's** together to make **Row A**. Make 6 **Row A's**.

Row A (make 6)

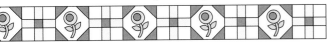

7. Sew 5 **Block B's** and 5 **Block A's** together to make **Row B**. Make 5 **Row B's**.

Row B (make 5)

8. Referring to **Quilt Top Diagram**, sew **Row A's** and **Row B's** together to make center section of quilt top.

9. Follow **Adding Squared Borders**, page 118, to sew **side**, then **top** and **bottom inner borders** to center section. Add **side**, then **top** and **bottom outer borders** to complete **Quilt Top**.

COMPLETING THE QUILT TOP

1. Follow **Quilting**, page 119, to mark, layer, and quilt, using **Quilting Diagram** as a suggestion. Our quilt is hand quilted.

2. Cut a 32" square of binding fabric. Follow **Binding**, page 123, to bind quilt using $2^1/2$"w bias binding with mitered corners.

Quilt Top Diagram

Quilting Diagram

POSY WALL HANGING

SKILL LEVEL: 1 2 3 4 5
BLOCK SIZE: 8" x 8"
WALL HANGING SIZE: 33" x 33"

YARDAGE REQUIREMENTS

Yardage is based on 45"w fabric.

- ☐ $7/8$ yd of white print
- ☐ $5/8$ yd of floral print
- ☐ $3/8$ yd of pink print
- ☐ $1/4$ yd of green solid
- ☐ $1/8$ yd of light pink solid
  $1^1/8$ yds for backing and hanging sleeve
  $5/8$ yd for binding
  35" x 35" batting

You will also need:
  paper-backed fusible web
  transparent monofilament thread for appliqué

CUTTING OUT THE PIECES

All measurements include a $1/4$" seam allowance. Follow Rotary Cutting, page 110, to cut fabric.

- **From white print:** ☐
  - Cut 2 **wide strips** $3^1/2$" x 21".
  - Cut 2 **strips** 9"w. From these strips, cut 5 **large squares** 9" x 9".
- **From floral print:** ☐
  - Cut 2 **top/bottom outer borders** $3^1/2$" x 32".
  - Cut 2 **side outer borders** $3^1/2$" x 26".
  - Cut 1 **strip** $2^1/2$" x 21".
  - Cut 2 **wide strips** $3^1/2$" x 21".
- **From pink print:** ☐
  - Cut 2 **strips** $3^1/2$"w. From these strips, cut 20 **medium squares** $3^1/2$" x $3^1/2$".
  - Cut 1 **narrow strip** $2^1/2$" x 21".
- **From green solid:** ☐
  - Cut 2 **top/bottom inner borders** $1^1/4$" x 26".
  - Cut 2 **strips** $1^1/4$" x $24^1/2$" for **side inner borders**.

PREPARING THE APPLIQUÉS

Use patterns, page 13, and follow Preparing Appliqué Pieces, page 116, to cut appliqués.

- **From light pink solid:** ☐
  - Cut 5 **Large Circles**.
- **From pink print:** ☐
  - Cut 5 **Small Circles**.
- **From green solid:** ☐
  - Cut 5 **Leaves**.
  - Cut 5 **Stems**.

ASSEMBLING THE WALL HANGING TOP

Follow Piecing and Pressing, page 113, to make wall hanging top.

1. Follow Steps 1 - 5 of **Assembling the Quilt Top** for **Pastel Posies Quilt**, pages 8-9, to make 5 **Block A's** and 4 **Block B's** (you will need 8 **Unit 1's** cut from 1 **Strip Set A** and 4 **Unit 2's** cut from 1 **Strip Set B** for **Block B's**).

Block A (make 5)   **Block B** (make 4)

2. Referring to **Wall Hanging Top Diagram**, sew **Block A's** and **Block B's** together to make center section of wall hanging top.
3. Sew **side**, then **top** and **bottom inner borders** to center section. Add **side**, then **top** and **bottom outer borders** to complete **Wall Hanging Top**.

COMPLETING THE WALL HANGING

1. Follow **Quilting**, page 119, to mark, layer, and quilt, using **Quilting Diagram**, page 9, as a suggestion. Our wall hanging is hand quilted.
2. Follow **Making a Hanging Sleeve**, page 125, to attach hanging sleeve to wall hanging.
3. Cut a 21" square of binding fabric. Follow **Binding**, page 123, to bind wall hanging using $2^1/2$"w bias binding with mitered corners.

Wall Hanging Top Diagram

PASTEL PILLOW SHAMS

PILLOW SHAM SIZE: 22" x 26" (without ruffle)

Instructions are for making 2 pillow shams.

YARDAGE REQUIREMENTS

Yardage is based on 45"w fabric.

- ☐ $2^1/8$ yds of floral print
- ☐ $1/2$ yd of white print
- ☐ $3/8$ yd of green solid
- ☐ $1/8$ yd of light pink solid
- ☐ $1/8$ yd of pink print
  $2^7/8$ yds for ruffle
  $1^5/8$ yds for sham top backings
  $5^1/2$ yds of 3"w bias strip for welting
  $5^1/2$ yds of $7/32$" cording

You will also need:
 paper-backed fusible web
 transparent monofilament thread for appliqué

CUTTING OUT THE PIECES

*Follow **Rotary Cutting**, page 110, to cut fabric.*

1. **From floral print:** ☐
   - Cut 4 rectangles $16^1/2$" x $22^1/2$" for **sham backs**.
   - Cut 4 **side outer borders** $3^3/4$" x $22^1/2$".
   - Cut 4 **top/bottom outer borders** $3^3/4$" x $20^1/2$".

2. **From white print:** ☐
   - Cut 2 rectangles 15" x 20" for **sham tops**.

3. **From green solid:** ☐
   - Cut 4 strips $1^1/4$"w. From strips, cut 2 **top/bottom inner borders** $1^1/4$" x 19" and 2 **side inner borders** $1^1/4$" x 16".

4. **From floral print for ruffle:**
   - Cut 14 strips 7"w.

MAKING THE SHAMS

1. Use patterns, page 13, and follow **Preparing Appliqué Pieces**, page 116, to cut 10 **Stems** and 10 **Leaves** from green solid, 10 **Large Circles** from light pink solid, and 12 **Small Circles** from pink print.
2. Referring to **Sham Top Diagram**, follow **Invisible Appliqué**, page 116, to stitch appliqués to each **sham top**. Trim **sham tops** to $14^1/2$" x 19".
3. Follow **Piecing and Pressing**, page 113, to sew **top, bottom**, then **side inner borders** to each **sham top**. Add **top, bottom**, then **side outer borders** to complete **Sham Tops**.

4. Follow **Quilting**, page 119, to mark, layer, and quilt. Our **Sham Tops** are hand quilted in the ditch around appliqués, with a diagonal grid on the background and inner borders, and with 2 outlines 1" apart on center of outer border.
5. Using a $1/2$" seam allowance, follow **Adding Welting to Pillow Top**, page 126, and **Adding Ruffle to Pillow Top**, page 127, to add welting and a 3"w ruffle to each sham top.
6. On each **sham back** piece, press one $22^1/2$" edge $1/2$" to the wrong side; press $1/2$" to the wrong side again and stitch in place.
7. For each **Sham Back**, place 2 **sham back** pieces right side up. Referring to **Fig. 1**, overlap finished edges and baste in place.

Fig. 1

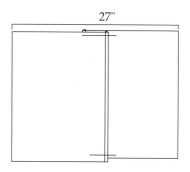

8. To complete each sham, place **Sham Back** and **Sham Top**, right sides together. Stitch through all layers as close as possible to welting. Cut corners diagonally; remove basting threads at opening. Turn **Sham** right side out; press.

Sham Top Diagram

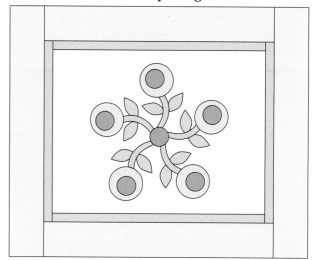

12

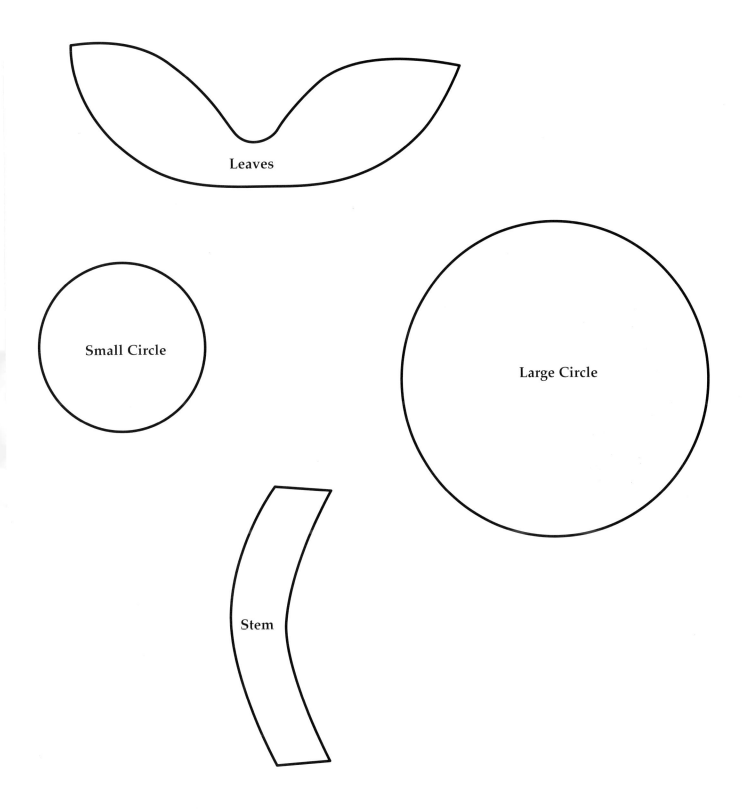

Leaves

Small Circle

Large Circle

Stem

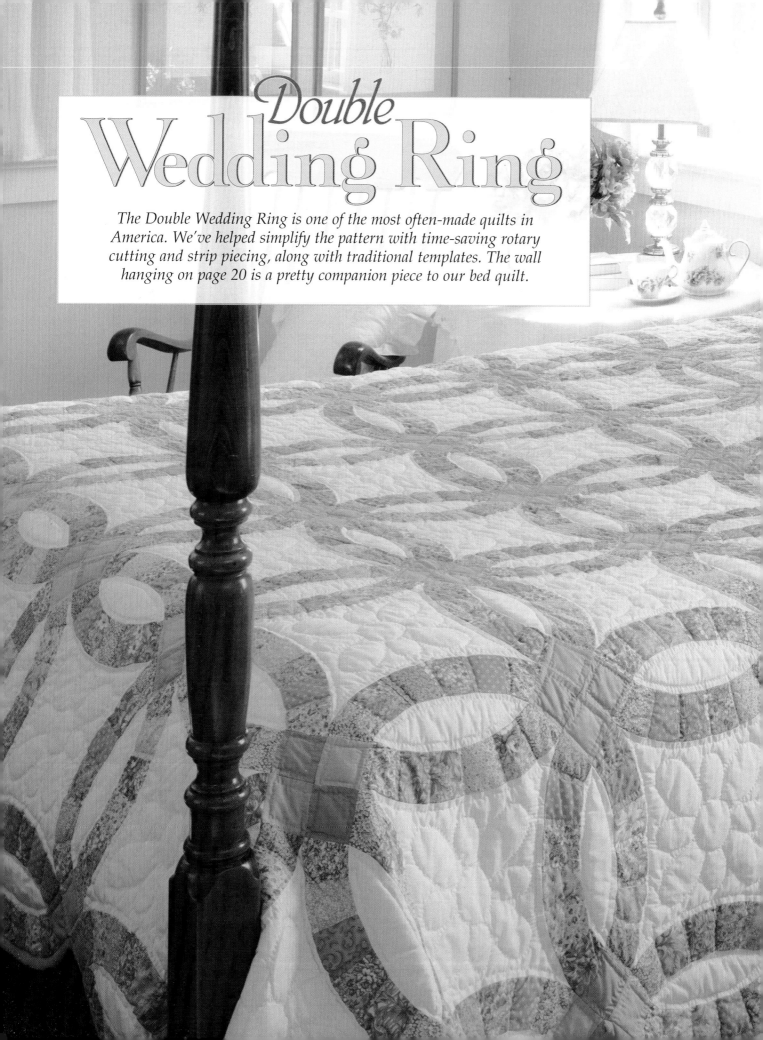

Double
Wedding Ring

The Double Wedding Ring is one of the most often-made quilts in America. We've helped simplify the pattern with time-saving rotary cutting and strip piecing, along with traditional templates. The wall hanging on page 20 is a pretty companion piece to our bed quilt.

DOUBLE WEDDING RING QUILT

SKILL LEVEL: 1 2 3 4 5
RING SIZE: 18" diameter
QUILT SIZE: 96" x 109"

YARDAGE REQUIREMENTS
Yardage is based on 45"w fabric.

- 8$1/2$ yds **total** of assorted pastel prints
- 6$1/2$ yds of white solid
- $5/8$ yd of peach solid
- $5/8$ yd of green solid
- 8$3/4$ yds for backing
- 1$1/4$ yds for binding
- 120" x 120" batting

ROTARY CUTTING
All measurements include a $1/4$" seam allowance. Follow
Rotary Cutting, page 110, to cut fabric.

1. **From pastel prints:**
   - Cut a total of 26 selvage-to-selvage **narrow strips** 2$1/2$"w.
   - Cut a total of 52 selvage-to-selvage **wide strips** 4$1/4$"w.

2. **From peach solid:**
   - Cut 8 selvage-to-selvage strips 2$1/2$"w. From these strips, cut 127 **squares** 2$1/2$" x 2$1/2$".

3. **From green solid:**
   - Cut 8 selvage-to-selvage strips 2$1/2$"w. From these strips, cut 127 **squares** 2$1/2$" x 2$1/2$".

ASSEMBLING THE STRIP SETS
Follow Piecing and Pressing, page 113, to make strip sets.

1. Beginning and ending with narrow strips, assemble 2 **narrow** and 4 **wide strips** in random color order to make **Strip Set**. Make 13 **Strip Sets**.

Strip Set (make 13)

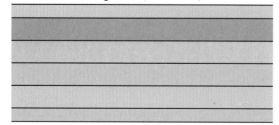

TEMPLATE CUTTING
Use patterns AA, AB, C, and D, page 22-23, and follow
Template Cutting, page 112, to cut fabric.

1. From 4 **Strip Sets**, use **Template AA** to cut out 254 **AA Units**, placing center line of template on seams as shown in **Fig. 1**.

Fig. 1

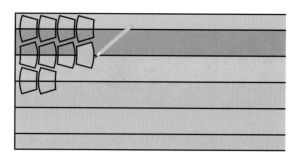

2. From remaining 9 **Strip Sets**, use **Template AB** to cut out 254 **AB Units** and 254 **Reversed AB Units**, placing center line of template on seams.

3. From white solid, cut 127 **C's** using **Template C** and 56 **D's** using **Template D**.

ASSEMBLING THE QUILT TOP
Follow Piecing and Pressing, page 113, to make
quilt top.

1. Assemble 1 **Reversed AB Unit**, 1 **AA Unit**, and 1 **AB Unit** to make **Unit 1**. Make 254 **Unit 1's**.

Unit 1 (make 254)

2. Assemble 2 **squares** and 1 **Unit 1** to make **Unit 2**. Make 127 **Unit 2's**.

Unit 2 (make 127)

16

3. (*Note:* For curved seams in Steps 3 - 8, match centers and pin at center and at dots, then match and pin between these points. Sew seam with convex edge on bottom next to feed dogs.) Assemble 1 **C** and 1 **Unit 1** to make **Unit 3**. Make 127 **Unit 3's**.

Unit 3 (make 127)

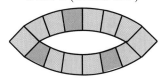

4. Assemble 1 **Unit 2** and 1 **Unit 3** to make **Unit 4**. Make 127 **Unit 4's**.

Unit 4 (make 127)

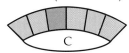

5. Assemble 4 **Unit 4's** and 1 **D** to make **Unit 5**. Make 28 **Unit 5's**.

Unit 5 (make 28)

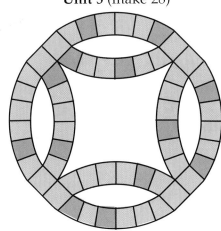

6. Assemble 2 **Unit 4's** and 1 **D** to make **Unit 6**. Make 2 **Unit 6's**.

Unit 6 (make 2)

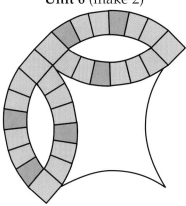

7. Assemble 1 **Unit 4** and 1 **D** to make **Unit 7**. Make 11 **Unit 7's**.

Unit 7 (make 11)

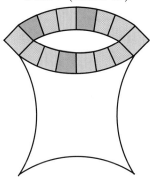

8. Follow **Assembly Diagram** to assemble **Unit 5's**, **Unit 6's**, **Unit 7's**, and remaining **D's** into horizontal **rows**. Assemble **rows** to complete **Quilt Top**.

COMPLETING THE QUILT

1. Follow **Quilting**, page 119, to mark, layer, and quilt, using **Quilting Diagram** as a suggestion. Our quilt is hand quilted using **Quilting Pattern A**, page 23.

2. Cut a 42" square of binding fabric. Follow **Making Continuous Bias Strip Binding**, page 123, to make approximately 14 yds of $2^1/_2$"w bias binding.

3. Follow Steps 1 and 2 of **Attaching Binding with Mitered Corners**, page 124, to pin binding to front of quilt. Sew binding to quilt, easing curves and leaving a 2" overlap. Trim off excess binding and stitch overlap in place. Fold binding over to quilt backing and pin in place, covering stitching line. Blindstitch binding to backing.

Quilting Diagram

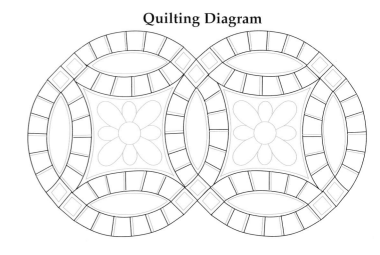

Assembly Diagram

18

DOUBLE WEDDING RING WALL HANGING

SKILL LEVEL: 1 2 3 4 5
RING SIZE: 18" diameter
WALL HANGING SIZE: 31" x 31"

YARDAGE REQUIREMENTS

Yardage is based on 45"w fabric.

- 1³/₄ yds **total** of assorted pastel prints
- 1 yd of white solid
- ¹/₈ yd of peach print
- ¹/₈ yd of blue print
  1¹/₄ yds for backing
  ³/₄ yd for binding
  35" x 35" batting

ROTARY CUTTING

All measurements include a ¹/₄" seam allowance. Follow Rotary Cutting, page 110, to cut fabric.

1. **From pastel prints:**
   - Cut a total of 2 selvage-to-selvage **strips** 2¹/₂"w.
   - Cut a total of 5 selvage-to-selvage **strips** 4¹/₄"w.

2. **From peach print:**
   - Cut 1 selvage-to-selvage strip 2¹/₂"w. From this strip, cut 12 **squares** 2¹/₂" x 2¹/₂".

3. **From blue print:**
   - Cut 1 selvage-to-selvage strip 2¹/₂"w. From this strip, cut 12 **squares** 2¹/₂" x 2¹/₂".

ASSEMBLING THE WALL HANGING TOP

Follow Piecing and Pressing, page 113, to make wall hanging top.

1. Beginning and ending with narrow strips, assemble **strips** in random color order to make 1 **Strip Set**.

Strip Set (make 1)

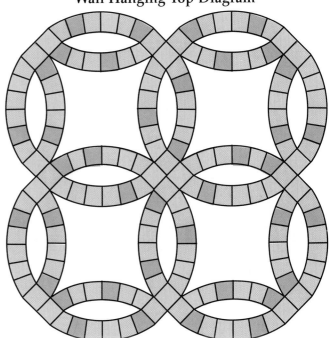

2. Referring to Steps 1 and 2 of **Template Cutting** for **Double Wedding Ring Quilt**, page 16, cut 24 **AA Units**, 24 **AB Units**, and 24 **Reversed AB Units**; From white solid, cut 12 **C's** using **Template C** and 4 **D's** using **Template D**.

3. Follow Steps 1 - 4 of **Assembling the Quilt Top** for **Double Wedding Ring Quilt**, pages 16-17, to make 12 **Unit 4's**.

4. Follow Steps 5 and 6 of **Assembling the Quilt Top** for **Double Wedding Ring Quilt**, page 17, to make 2 **Unit 5's** and 2 **Unit 6's**.

5. Assemble **Unit 5's** and **Unit 6's** to complete **Wall Hanging Top**.

COMPLETING THE WALL HANGING

1. Follow **Quilting**, page 119, to mark, layer, and quilt, using **Quilting Diagram** as a suggestion. Our wall hanging is hand quilted using **Quilting Pattern B**, page 22.

3. Cut a 22" square of binding fabric. Follow **Making Continuous Bias Strip Binding**, page 123, to make approximately 5 yds of 2¹/₂"w bias binding.

4. Follow Step 3 of **Completing the Quilt** for **Double Wedding Ring Quilt**, page 18, to attach binding to wall hanging.

Wall Hanging Top Diagram

Quilting Diagram

21

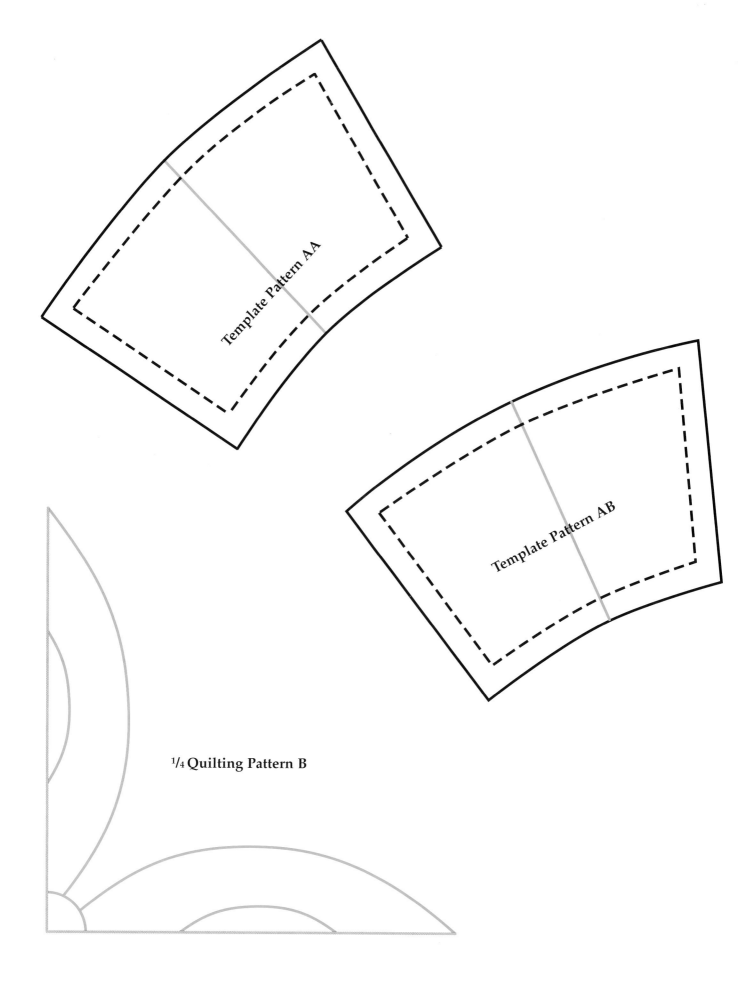

Template Pattern AA

Template Pattern AB

¼ Quilting Pattern B

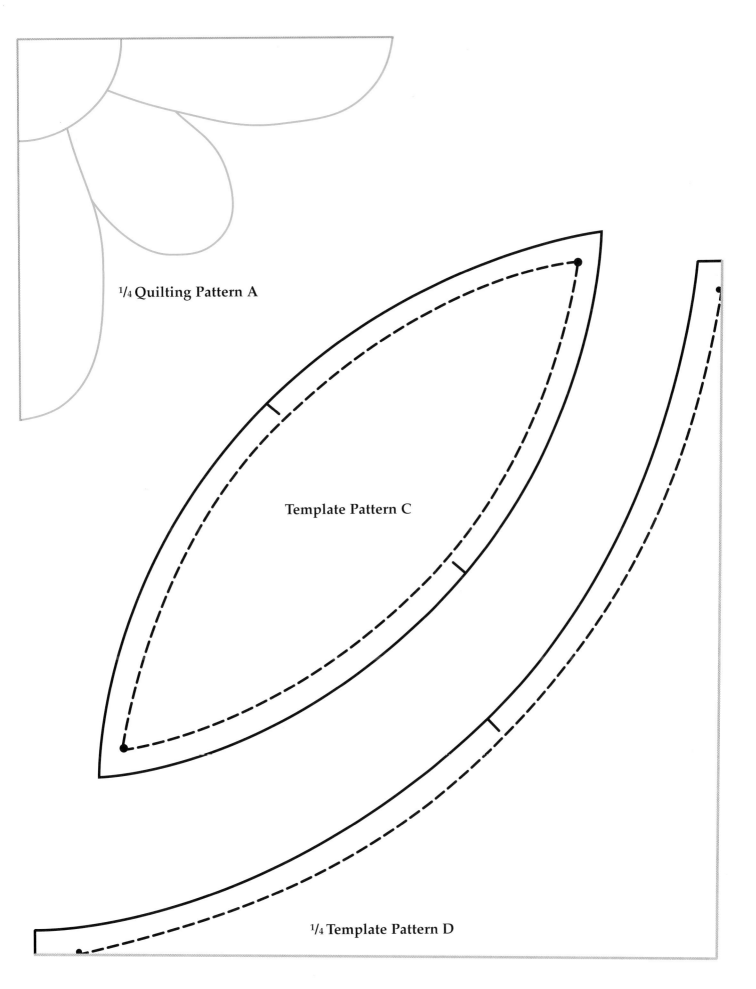

¼ Quilting Pattern A

Template Pattern C

¼ Template Pattern D

23

Floral Nine-Patch

Even a basic pattern like the Nine-Patch can blossom into a contemporary beauty when pieced with daringly coordinated fabrics. For our Floral Nine-Patch quilt, we selected a bold print and accented it with several smaller prints in complementary shades. Simple strip-set sashing and plain setting squares offset the blocks.

FLORAL NINE-PATCH QUILT

SKILL LEVEL: 1 2 3 4 5
BLOCK SIZE: 9" x 9"
QUILT SIZE: 86" x 98"

YARDAGE REQUIREMENTS

Yardage is based on 45"w fabric.

- $4^1/_2$ yds of large floral print
- $3^7/_8$ yds of green print
- $3^5/_8$ yds of purple print
- $1^7/_8$ yds of white print
  8 yds for backing
  1 yd for binding
  120" x 120" batting

CUTTING OUT THE PIECES

All measurements include a ¼" seam allowance. Follow
Rotary Cutting, *page 110, to cut fabric.*

1. **From large floral print:**
   - Cut 13 **wide strips** $3^1/_2$"w.
   - Cut 4 strips $3^1/_2$"w. From these strips, cut 42 **sashing squares** $3^1/_2$" x $3^1/_2$".
   - Cut 2 lengthwise **top/bottom wide borders** $8^1/_2$" x $85^1/_2$".
   - Cut 2 lengthwise **side wide borders** $8^1/_2$" x $81^1/_2$".

2. **From green print:**
   - Cut 18 **narrow strips** $1^1/_2$"w.
   - Cut 2 lengthwise **side outer borders** $2^1/_2$" x $97^1/_2$".
   - Cut 2 lengthwise **top/bottom outer borders** $2^1/_2$" x $89^1/_2$".

3. **From purple print:**
   - Cut 11 **wide strips** $3^1/_2$"w.
   - Cut 2 lengthwise **side inner borders** $1^1/_2$" x 79".
   - Cut 2 lengthwise **top/bottom inner borders** $1^1/_2$" x $69^1/_2$".

4. **From white print:**
   - Cut 36 **narrow strips** $1^1/_2$"w.

ASSEMBLING THE QUILT TOP

Follow ***Piecing and Pressing****, page 113, to make quilt top.*

1. Sew 3 **wide strips** together to make **Strip Set A**. Make 5 **Strip Set A's**. Cut across **Strip Set A's** at $3^1/_2$" intervals to make 60 **Unit 1's**.

Strip Set A (make 5)   **Unit 1** (make 60)

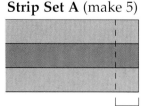

$3^1/_2$"

2. Sew 3 **wide strips** together to make **Strip Set B**. Make 3 **Strip Set B's**. Cut across **Strip Set B's** at $3^1/_2$" intervals to make 30 **Unit 2's**.

Strip Set B (make 3)   **Unit 2** (make 30)

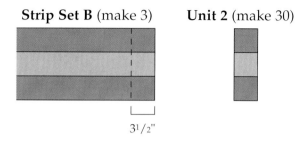

$3^1/_2$"

3. Sew 2 **Unit 1's** and 1 **Unit 2** together to make **Block**. Make 30 **Blocks**.

Block (make 30)

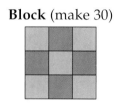

4. Sew 3 **narrow strips** together to make **Strip Set C**. Make 18 **Strip Set C's**. Cut across **Strip Set C's** at $9^1/_2$" intervals to make 71 **Sashing Units**.

Strip Set C (make 18)   **Sashing Unit** (make 71)

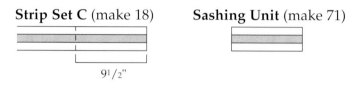

$9^1/_2$"

5. Sew 5 **Blocks** and 6 **Sashing Units** together to make **Row**. Make 6 **Rows**.

Row (make 6)

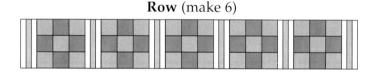

6. Sew 6 **sashing squares** and 5 **Sashing Units** together to make **Sashing Row**. Make 7 **Sashing Rows**.

Sashing Row (make 7)

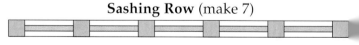

7. Referring to **Quilt Top Diagram**, sew **Sashing Rows** and **Rows** together to make center section of quilt top.

8. Follow **Adding Squared Borders**, page 118, to sew **side**, then **top** and **bottom inner borders** to center section. Repeat to add **wide borders**, then **outer borders** to complete **Quilt Top**.

COMPLETING THE QUILT

1. Follow **Quilting**, page 119, to mark, layer, and quilt, using **Quilting Diagram** as a suggestion. Our quilt is hand quilted.
2. Cut a 33" square of binding fabric. Follow **Binding**, page 123, to bind quilt using $2^1/2$"w bias binding with overlapping corners.

Quilting Diagram

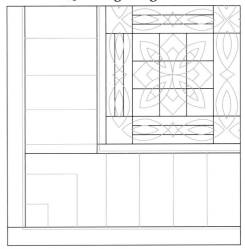

Quilt Top Diagram

Paramount Star

This classic blue medallion-style quilt features a central star design, sawtooth borders, LeMoyne Star blocks, and appliquéd leaves and vines. Handy shortcuts make the piecing and appliqué go quickly.

PARAMOUNT STAR QUILT

SKILL LEVEL: 1 2 3 4 5
QUILT SIZE: 98" x 111"

YARDAGE REQUIREMENTS

Yardage is based on 45"w fabric.

- ☐ $10^7/8$ yds of white solid
- ◼ $4^1/4$ yds of dark blue solid
- ◼ $2^3/4$ yds of blue print
- ◻ $2^1/8$ yds of light blue solid
  $8^3/4$ yds for backing
  1 yd for binding
  120" x 120" batting

You will also need:
  transparent monofilament thread for appliqué
  $2^3/8$ yds of 19"w water-soluble stabilizer
  $3/8$" bias pressing bar

CUTTING OUT THE PIECES

All measurements include a $1/4$" seam allowance. Follow Rotary Cutting, page 110, to cut fabric unless otherwise indicated. To simplify quilt top assembly, group all pieces for each of the quilt sections listed into separate stacks.

1. **From white solid:** ☐

(for Feathered Star Medallion)
- Cut 1 **rectangle** 10" x 20" for triangle-squares.
- Cut 4 **medium squares** $2^7/8$" x $2^7/8$".
- Cut 2 squares $4^5/8$" x $4^5/8$". Cut squares twice diagonally to make 8 **medium triangles**.
- Cut 4 **large squares** $7^3/4$" x $7^3/4$".
- Cut 1 square $11^1/2$" x $11^1/2$". Cut square twice diagonally to make 4 **large triangles**.
- Cut 1 strip 2"w. From this strip, cut 8 squares 2" x 2". Cut each square once diagonally to make 16 **small triangles**.

(for Sawtooth Borders)
- Cut 13 **rectangles** 14" x 16" for triangle-squares.
- Cut 10 **squares** $1^5/8$" x $1^5/8$".

(for Vine Borders)
- Cut 4 selvage-to-selvage strips 6" x 41" for **inner vine borders**.
- Cut 2 lengthwise strips 6" x $83^3/4$" for **top/bottom outer vine borders**.
- Cut 2 lengthwise strips 6" x $97^1/4$" for **side outer vine borders**.

(for LeMoyne Star Blocks)
- Cut 2 selvage-to-selvage strips $2^1/8$"w. From these strips, cut 32 **small squares** $2^1/8$" x $2^1/8$".
- Cut 1 selvage-to-selvage strip $3^1/2$"w. From this strip, cut 8 squares $3^1/2$" x $3^1/2$". Cut each square twice diagonally to make 32 **small triangles**.
- Cut 7 selvage-to-selvage strips $3^1/4$"w. From these strips, cut 80 **medium squares** $3^1/4$" x $3^1/4$".
- Cut 3 selvage-to-selvage strips $5^1/8$"w. From these strips, cut 20 squares $5^1/8$" x $5^1/8$". Cut each square twice diagonally to make 80 **medium triangles**.

(for Setting Pieces)
- Cut 3 selvage-to-selvage strips $14^3/4$"w. From these strips, cut 5 squares $14^3/4$" x $14^3/4$". Cut each square twice diagonally to make 20 **setting triangles** (you will need 18 and have 2 left over).
- Cut 2 squares $14^3/8$" x $14^3/8$". Cut each square once diagonally to make 4 **corner setting triangles**.

2. **From dark blue solid:** ◼

(for Feathered Star Medallion)
- Use **Template A** pattern, page 37, and follow **Template Cutting**, page 112, to cut 8 **A's**.

(for Sawtooth Borders)
- Cut 8 **rectangles** 14" x 16" for triangle-squares.

(for Vine Borders)
- Cut 1 **square** 27" x 27" for bias strip.
- Cut 3 selvage-to-selvage **strips** 4"w for leaf appliqués.

(for LeMoyne Star Blocks)
- Cut 4 selvage-to-selvage **strips** $1^5/8$"w.
- Cut 16 selvage-to-selvage **strips** $2^1/2$"w.

3. **From blue print:** ◼

(for Feathered Star Medallion)
- Cut 1 selvage-to-selvage **strip** $2^1/8$"w.

(for Setting Pieces)
- Cut 2 squares 20" x 20". Cut each square once diagonally to make 4 **large setting triangles**.
- Cut 3 selvage-to-selvage strips 10"w. From these strips, cut 10 **setting squares** 10" x 10".
- Cut 2 selvage-to-selvage strips $14^3/4$"w. From these strips, cut 4 squares $14^3/4$" x $14^3/4$". Cut each square twice diagonally to make 16 **setting triangles**.
- Cut 2 squares $7^5/8$" x $7^5/8$". Cut each square once diagonally to make 4 **small setting triangles**.

4. **From light blue solid:** ◻

(for Feathered Star Medallion)
- Cut 1 **rectangle** 10" x 20" for triangle-squares.
- Cut 1 selvage-to-selvage **strip** $1^5/8$"w.

(for Sawtooth Borders)
- Cut 5 **rectangles** 14" x 16" for triangle-squares.

(for Vine Borders)
- Cut 1 **square** 18" x 18" for bias strip.
- Cut 2 selvage-to-selvage **strips** 4"w for leaf appliqués.

MAKING THE QUILT TOP SECTIONS

Follow Piecing and Pressing, page 113, to make quilt top sections.

FEATHERED STAR MEDALLION

1. Referring to **Fig. 1**, align the 45° marking (shown in pink) on the rotary cutting ruler along the lower edge of light blue solid **strip**. Cut along right edge of ruler to cut 1 end of **strip** at a 45° angle.

Fig. 1

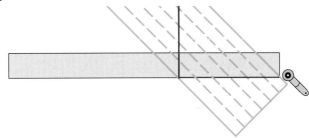

2. Turn cut strip 180° on mat and align the 45° marking on the rotary cutting ruler along the lower edge of the strip. Align the previously cut 45° edge with the 1⅝" marking on the ruler. Cut strip at 1⅝" intervals as shown in **Fig. 2** to cut a total of 8 **small diamonds**. Set aside for use in Step 12.

Fig. 2

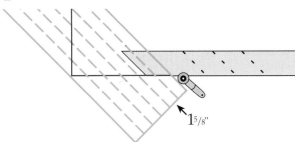

Using blue print **strip**, repeat Steps 1 and 2, cutting strip at 2⅛" intervals to make a total of 8 **large diamonds**.

Follow **Working with Set-in Seams**, page 115, to assemble 8 **large diamonds**, 4 **medium squares**, and 4 **medium triangles** to make **Star Block**.

Star Block (make 1)

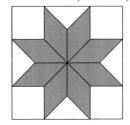

To make triangle-squares, place white solid and light blue solid **rectangles** right sides together and follow Steps 1 - 3 of **Making Triangle-Squares**, page 114, to draw a grid of 36 squares 2" x 2" (**Fig. 3**). Referring to **Fig. 3** for stitching direction, follow Steps 4 - 6 of **Making Triangle-Squares** to make a total of 72 **triangle-squares**.

Fig. 3

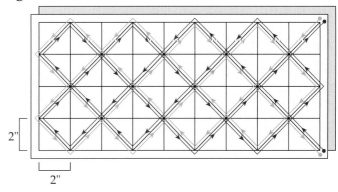

triangle-square (make 72)

6. Assemble 1 **small triangle** and 4 **triangle-squares** to make **Unit 1**. Make 4 **Unit 1's**.

Unit 1 (make 4)

7. Assemble 1 **large triangle** and 1 **Unit 1** to make **Unit 2**, leaving portion of seam shown in pink unstitched at this time. Make 4 **Unit 2's**.

Unit 2 (make 4)

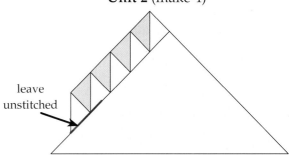

leave unstitched

8. Assemble 5 **triangle-squares** and 1 **small triangle** to make **Unit 3**. Make 4 **Unit 3's**.

Unit 3 (make 4)

9. Assemble 1 **Unit 2**, 1 **Unit 3**, and 1 **A** to make **Unit 4**, leaving portion of seam shown in pink unstitched at this time. Make 4 **Unit 4's**.

Unit 4 (make 4)

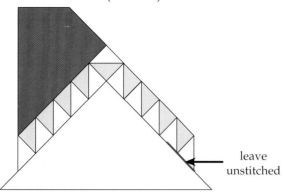

leave unstitched

10. Assemble 1 **A** and 1 **medium triangle** to make **Unit 5**. Make 4 **Unit 5's**.

Unit 5 (make 4)

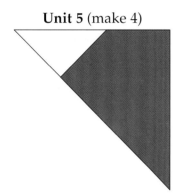

11. Assemble 1 **Unit 4** and 1 **Unit 5** to make **Unit 6**. Make 4 **Unit 6's**.

Unit 6 (make 4)

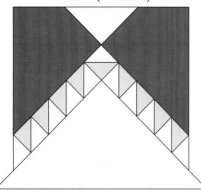

12. Assemble 1 **small diamond** and 1 **small triangle** to make **Unit 7**. Make 4 **Unit 7's**. Assemble 1 **small triangle** and 1 **small diamond** to make **Unit 8**. Make 4 **Unit 8's**.

Unit 7 (make 4)   Unit 8 (make 4)

13. Assemble 1 **Unit 7** and 5 **triangle-squares** to ma **Unit 9**. Make 4 **Unit 9's**.

Unit 9 (make 4)

14. Assemble 4 **triangle-squares** and 1 **Unit 8** to ma **Unit 10**. Make 4 **Unit 10's**.

Unit 10 (make 4)

15. Assemble 1 **Unit 9**, 1 **Unit 10**, and 1 **large square** to make **Corner Block**. Make 4 **Corner Blocks**.

Corner Block (make 4)

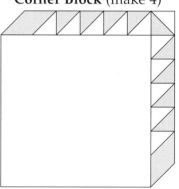

16. Assemble **Star Block**, **Unit 6's**, and **Corner Blocks** into rows (**Fig. 4**). Sew long seams to join rows, then finish sewing portions of seams left unstitched in Steps 7 and 9 to complete **Feathered Star Medallion**.

Fig. 4

32

SAWTOOTH BORDERS

1. To make triangle-squares, place 1 white solid and 1 light blue solid **rectangle** right sides together and follow Steps 1 - 3 of **Making Triangle-Squares**, page 114, to draw a grid of 42 squares 2" x 2" (**Fig. 5**). Referring to **Fig. 5** for stitching direction, follow Steps 4 - 6 of **Making Triangle-Squares** to make 84 triangle-squares. Repeat with remaining 4 light blue solid **rectangles** and 4 of the white **rectangles** to make a total of 420 **triangle-square A's** (you will need 414 and have 6 left over).

Fig. 5

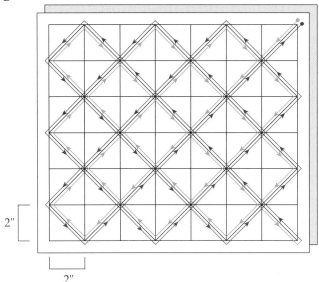

2"

2"

triangle-square A (make 420)

Repeat Step 1 using 8 white solid and 8 dark blue solid **rectangles** to make 672 **triangle-square B's**.

triangle-square B (make 672)

Referring to **Quilt Top Diagram**, page 36, for arrangement of **triangle-squares** and **squares**, assemble the numbers of pieces indicated in the **Sawtooth Border Assembly** table to make **Sawtooth Borders**.

Sawtooth Border Assembly

Name of Borders	Number of Borders	Number of Pieces per Border	
		Triangle-Squares	Squares
1st (Inner) Side	2	22A	–
1st Top/Bottom	2	23A	1
2nd Side	2	34A	–
2nd Top/Bottom	2	34A	2
3rd Side	2	46A	–
3rd Top/Bottom	2	48A	–
4th Side	2	84B	–
4th Top/Bottom	2	72B	2
5th Side	2	96B	–
5th Top/Bottom	2	86B	–

VINE BORDERS

1. To make **Vine Appliqués**, use light blue solid **square** and follow Steps 1 - 7 of **Making Continuous Bias Strip Binding**, page 123, to make a $1^{1}/_{4}$"w bias strip. Cut bias strip into 4 pieces approximately 50"l. Use dark blue solid **square** to make a $1^{1}/_{4}$"w bias strip. Cut bias strip into 2 pieces approximately 100"l and 2 pieces approximately 110"l.

2. Fold 1 bias strip in half lengthwise with wrong sides together; do not press. Stitch $1/_{4}$" from long raw edge to form a tube; trim seam allowance to $1/_{8}$". Repeat with remaining bias strips.

3. Place bias pressing bar inside 1 bias tube. Center seam and press as you move bar down length of tube. Repeat with remaining bias tubes to complete **Vine Appliqués**.

4. To make **Leaf Appliqués**, cut 5 strips of stabilizer 4" x 42". Use a permanent fabric marker to trace **Leaf** pattern, page 37, onto stabilizer strips, leaving at least $1/_{2}$" between leaves. Place stabilizer strips on right side of 4"w fabric **strips**. Stitch on marked lines. Trim fabric and stabilizer to within $1/_{4}$" of stitching line; clip curves and points. To make opening for turning, cut a slit through stabilizer only. Turn right side out and press with a dry iron. Make 36 light blue solid and 76 dark blue solid **Leaf Appliqués**.

5. Referring to **Quilt Top Diagram**, page 36, for placement, follow **Mock Hand Appliqué**, page 117, to stitch **Vine** and **Leaf Appliqués** to **inner** and **outer vine borders**.

LeMOYNE STAR BLOCKS

1. Using $1^{5}/_{8}$"w **strips** and cutting at $1^{5}/_{8}$" intervals, follow Steps 1 and 2 of **Feathered Star Medallion**, page 30, to cut 64 **diamonds**. Use **diamonds**, **small squares**, and **small triangles** and follow Step 4 of **Feathered Star Medallion**, page 31, to make 8 **Small Star Blocks**.

2. Using $2^1/2$"w **strips** and cutting at $2^1/2$" intervals, follow Steps 1 and 2 of **Feathered Star Medallion**, page 30, to cut 160 **diamonds**. Use **diamonds**, **medium squares**, and **medium triangles** and follow Step 4 of **Feathered Star Medallion**, page 31, to make 20 **Large Star Blocks**.

ASSEMBLING THE QUILT TOP
*Follow **Piecing and Pressing**, page 113, to make quilt top.*

1. (*Note:* Refer to **Center Medallion Diagram** for Steps 1 - 4.) Sew **1st Side Sawtooth Borders**, then **1st Top** and **Bottom Sawtooth Borders** to **Feathered Star Medallion**. Sew **large setting triangles** to sides of medallion.

2. Sew **2nd Side Sawtooth Borders**, then **2nd Top** and **Bottom Sawtooth Borders** to medallion.

3. Sew 1 **Small Star Block** to each end of **top** and **bottom inner vine borders**. Sew **side**, then **top** and **bottom inner vine borders** to medallion.

4. Sew **3rd Side Sawtooth Borders**, then **3rd Top** and **Bottom Sawtooth Borders** to medallion to complete **Center Medallion**.

Center Medallion Diagram

5. Assemble 2 blue print **small setting triangles**, 3 blue print **setting triangles**, 4 **Large Star Blocks**, 3 blue print **setting squares**, and 2 white **setting triangles** to make **Unit 11**. Make 2 **Unit 11's**.

Unit 11 (make 2)

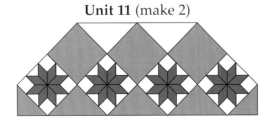

6. Assemble 5 blue print **setting triangles**, 4 **Large Star Blocks**, and 3 white **setting triangles** to make **Unit 12**. Make 2 **Unit 12's**.

Unit 12 (make 2)

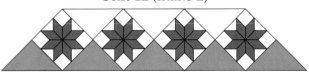

7. Assemble 1 **setting square**, 1 **Large Star Block**, 2 white **setting triangles**, and 1 **corner setting triangle** to make **Unit 13**. Make 2 **Unit 13's**.

Unit 13 (make 2)

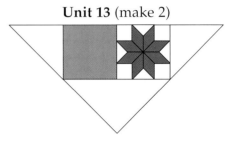

8. Assemble 1 **Large Star Block**, 1 **setting square**, 2 white **setting triangles**, and 1 **corner setting triangle** to make **Unit 14**. Make 2 **Unit 14's**.

Unit 14 (make 2)

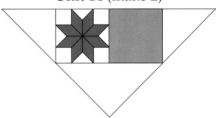

9. Referring to **Assembly Diagram**, sew **Unit 11's** to top and bottom of **Center Medallion**. Add **Unit 12's** to sides, then **Unit 13's** and **Unit 14's** to appropriate corners to complete center section of quilt top.

Assembly Diagram

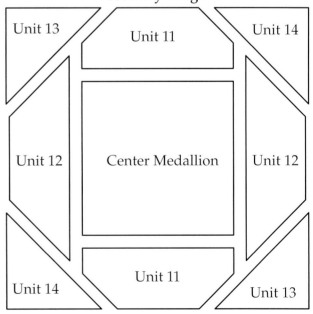

34

10. (*Note:* Refer to **Quilt Top Diagram**, page 36, when adding remaining borders.) Sew **4th Side Sawtooth Borders**, then **4th Top** and **Bottom Sawtooth Borders** to center section of quilt top.

11. Sew 1 **Small Star Block** to each end of **top** and **bottom outer vine borders**. Sew **side**, then **top** and **bottom outer vine borders** to center section of quilt top.

12. Sew **5th Side Sawtooth Borders**, then **5th Top** and **Bottom Sawtooth Borders** to center section of quilt top to complete **Quilt Top**.

COMPLETING THE QUILT

1. Follow **Quilting**, page 119, to mark, layer, and quilt, using **Quilting Diagram** as a suggestion. Our quilt is hand quilted using classic feather, feather wreath, and shell designs.

2. Cut a 36" square of binding fabric. Follow **Binding**, page 123, to bind quilt using $2^1/2$"w bias binding with mitered corders.

Quilting Diagram

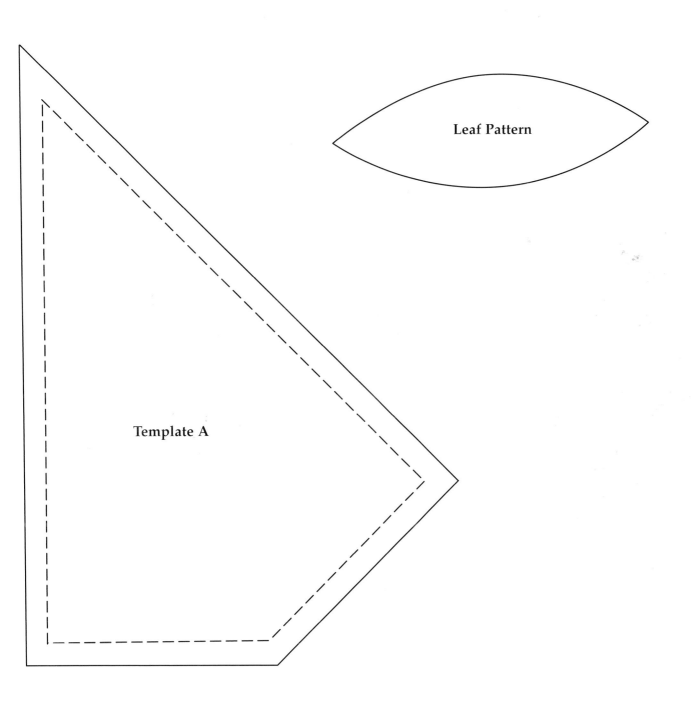

Leaf Pattern

Template A

Baskets Abloom

Perfect for a young girl's bedroom, the dainty floral baskets on this quilt finish faster with rotary cutting and strip piecing techniques. The coordinating patchwork pillow with a gingham ruffle is quick to complete, as well.

BASKETS ABLOOM QUILT

SKILL LEVEL: 1 2 3 4 5
BLOCK SIZE: $10^1/2$" x $10^1/2$"
QUILT SIZE: 81" x 95"

YARDAGE REQUIREMENTS

Yardage is based on 45"w fabric.

- $3^3/8$ yds of large yellow print
- $2^5/8$ yds of floral with blue background
- $2^7/8$ yds of pink check
- $1^7/8$ yds of white print
- $5/8$ yd of green print
- $3/8$ yd of pink print
- $3/8$ yd of small yellow print
  $7^1/2$ yds for backing
  1 yd for binding
  90" x 108" batting

CUTTING OUT THE PIECES

All measurements include a $^1/4$" seam allowance. Follow
***Rotary Cutting**, page 110, to cut fabric.*

1. **From large yellow print:**
   - Cut 2 strips $8^1/2$" x 99" for **side outer borders**.
   - Cut 2 strips $8^1/2$" x 68" for **top/bottom outer borders**.
   - Cut 4 selvage-to-selvage **strips** $2^1/4$"w.

2. **From floral with blue background:**
   - Cut 4 selvage-to-selvage strips 11"w. From these strips, cut 12 **setting squares** 11" x 11".
   - Cut 2 selvage-to-selvage strips $16^1/8$"w. From these strips, cut 4 squares $16^1/8$" x $16^1/8$". Cut squares twice diagonally to make 16 **side setting triangles** (you will need 14 and have 2 left over).

side setting triangle (cut 16)

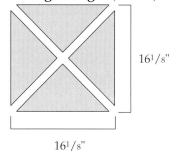

$16^1/8$"

$16^1/8$"

- Cut 2 squares $8^1/4$" x $8^1/4$". Cut squares once diagonally to make 4 **corner setting triangles**.

corner setting triangle (cut 4)

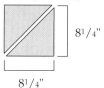

$8^1/4$"

$8^1/4$"

3. **From pink check:**
   - Cut 2 strips $2^1/2$" x 82" for **side inner borders**.
   - Cut 2 strips $2^1/2$" x 64" for **top/bottom inner borders**.
   - Cut 4 selvage-to-selvage **strips** $2^1/4$"w.

4. **From white print:**
   - Cut 8 selvage-to-selvage strips 4"w. From these strips, cut 40 **small rectangles** 4" x $7^1/2$".
   - Cut 2 selvage-to-selvage strips 4"w. From these strips, cut 20 **squares** 4" x 4".
   - Cut 2 selvage-to-selvage strips $4^3/4$"w. From this strip, cut 10 squares $4^3/4$" x $4^3/4$". Cut squares twice diagonally to make 40 **triangles**.

triangle (cut 40)

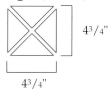

$4^3/4$"

$4^3/4$"

- Cut 1 **large rectangle** 10" x 23" for triangle-squares.

5. **From green print:**
   - Cut 2 selvage-to-selvage strips $4^3/8$"w. From these strips, cut 10 squares $4^3/8$" x $4^3/8$". Cut squares once diagonally to make 20 **triangles**.

triangle (cut 20)

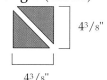

$4^3/8$"

$4^3/8$"

- Cut 1 **large rectangle** 10" x 23" for triangle-square

6. **From pink print:**
   - Cut 4 selvage-to-selvage **strips** $2^1/4$"w.

7. **From small yellow print:**
   - Cut 4 selvage-to-selvage **strips** $2^1/4$"w.

ASSEMBLING THE QUILT TOP

*Follow **Piecing and Pressing**, page 113, to make quilt top.*

1. To make triangle-squares, place green and white **large rectangles** right sides together. Referring to **Fig. 1**, follow Steps 1 - 3 of **Making Triangle-Squares**, page 114, to draw a grid of 10 squares $4^3/8$" x $4^3/8$".

Fig. 1

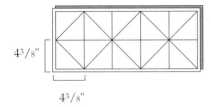

Referring to **Fig. 2** for sewing directions, follow Steps 4 - 6 of **Making Triangle-Squares**, page 114, to make a total of 20 **triangle-squares**.

Fig. 2

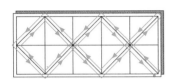

triangle-square (make 20)

2. To cut parallelograms, refer to **Fig. 3** and place 2 matching **strips** right sides together on mat. Align the 45° marking on the rotary cutting ruler (shown in pink) along lower right edge of strips. Cut along right side of ruler to cut 1 end of both strips at a 45° angle.

Fig. 3

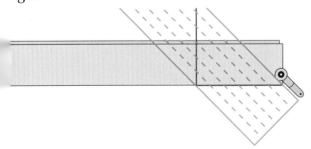

3. Turn cut strips 180° on mat and align the 45° marking on the rotary cutting ruler along lower left edge of strip. Align the previously cut 45° edge at the 3" marking on the ruler. Cut strips at 3" intervals as shown in **Fig 4**.

Fig. 4

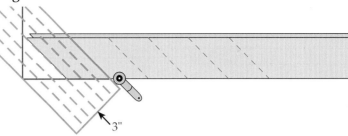

4. Repeat Steps 2 and 3 with remaining **strips** to cut a total of 20 parallelograms each from large yellow print, pink check, pink print, and small yellow print.

5. Follow Step 1 of **Working with Set-in Seams**, page 115, to assemble parallelograms to make 10 each of **Unit 1a**, **Unit 1b**, **Unit 1c**, and **Unit 1d**. Assemble **Units 1a, 1b, 1c,** and **1d** as shown to make 4 each of **Unit 2a** and **Unit 2d**; make 6 each of **Unit 2b** and **Unit 2c**. (*Note:* In remaining steps, **Unit 2a** will represent all **Unit 2** combinations.)

Unit 1a (make 10)	Unit 1b (make 10)	Unit 1c (make 10)	Unit 1d (make 10)
Unit 2a (make 4)	Unit 2b (make 6)	Unit 2c (make 6)	Unit 2d (make 4)

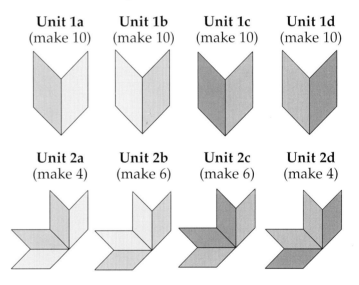

6. Follow Steps 2 and 3 of **Working with Set-in Seams**, page 115, to assemble 1 **square** and 1 **Unit 2** as shown to make **Unit 3**. Make 20 **Unit 3's**. Assemble 2 **triangles** and 1 **Unit 3** as shown to make **Unit 4**. Make 20 **Unit 4's**.

Unit 3 (make 20)   **Unit 4** (make 20)

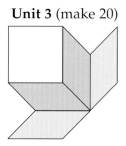 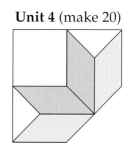

7. Assemble 1 **Unit 4** and 1 **triangle** as shown to make **Unit 5**. Make 20 **Unit 5's**.

Unit 5 (make 20)

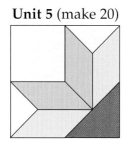

8. Assemble 1 **Unit 5** and 1 **small rectangle** as shown to make **Unit 6**. Make 20 **Unit 6's**.

Unit 6 (make 20)

9. Assemble 1 **small rectangle** and 1 **triangle-square** as shown to make **Unit 7**. Make 20 **Unit 7's**.

Unit 7 (make 20)

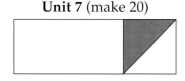

10. Assemble 1 **Unit 6** and 1 **Unit 7** as shown to make **Block**. Make 4 each of **Block A** and **Block D**; make 6 each of **Block B** and **Block C**.

Block A (make 4)   **Block B** (make 6)

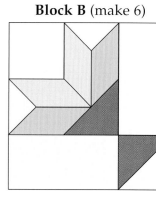

Block C (make 6)   **Block D** (make 4)

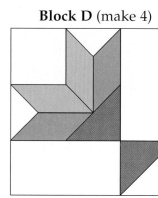

11. Refer to **Assembly Diagram** to assemble **Blocks**, **setting squares**, **side setting triangles**, and **corner setting triangles** into rows; sew rows together to complete center section of quilt top.

12. Follow **Adding Squared Borders**, page 118, and **Quilt Top Diagram**, page 43, to add **top**, **bottom**, and then **side inner borders**. Add **top**, **bottom**, and then **side outer borders** to complete **Quilt Top**.

COMPLETING THE QUILT

1. Follow **Quilting**, page 119, and **Quilting Diagram**, page 43, and use **Flower** and **Serpentine Quilting Pattern**s, page 45, to mark, layer, and quilt. Our quilt is hand quilted.

2. Cut a 36" square of binding fabric. Follow **Making Continuous Bias Strip Binding**, page 123, to make approximately $10^1/_2$ yds of $2^1/_2$"w bias binding.

3. Follow **Attaching Binding with Mitered Corners**, page 124, to attach binding to quilt.

Quilt Top Diagram

Assembly Diagram

Quilting Diagram

RUFFLED PATCHWORK PILLOW

SIZE: 15" x 15" (without ruffle)

YARDAGE REQUIREMENTS:

Yardage is based on 45"w fabric.

- 25 **total** squares $3^1/_2$" x $3^1/_2$" (our pillow uses fabric scraps from the **Baskets Abloom Quilt**)
- $^5/_8$ yd for ruffle
- $15^1/_2$" x $15^1/_2$" square for backing

You will also need:
- polyester fiberfill

MAKING THE PILLOW

*Follow **Piecing and Pressing**, page 113, to make pillow top.*

Referring to photo, assemble 5 **squares** to make **Row**. Make 5 **Rows**. Assemble **Rows** to make **Pillow Top**.

From fabric for ruffle, cut four strips $3^1/_2$" wide.

Follow **Pillow Finishing**, page 126, to complete pillow with a 3" ruffle.

Flower Quilting Pattern

Serpentine Quilting Pattern

Crown of Thorns

Patterns with Biblical themes have long been a favorite among quilters. To make this simple quilt even easier, our instructions call for rotary cutting and strip piecing, and a grid method makes the triangle-squares a breeze to put together!

CROWN OF THORNS QUILT

SKILL LEVEL: 1 2 3 4 5
BLOCK SIZE: 10" x 10"
QUILT SIZE: 76" x 76"

YARDAGE REQUIREMENTS

Yardage is based on 45"w fabric.

- ☐ 5¹/₂ yds of white
- ◼ 2 yds of green
- ◼ 1¹/₄ yds of red
- ◻ ¹/₄ yd of yellow
  4³/₄ yds for backing
  1 yd of green for binding
  81" x 96" batting

CUTTING OUT THE PIECES

All measurements include a ¹/₄" seam allowance. Follow **Rotary Cutting**, *page 110, to cut fabric.*

1. **From white:** ☐
   - Cut 7 selvage-to-selvage strips 2¹/₂"w.
   - Cut 7 selvage-to-selvage strips 10¹/₂"w. From these strips, cut a total of 25 **setting squares** 10¹/₂" x 10¹/₂".

setting square (cut 25)

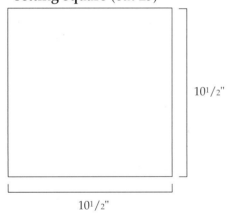

10¹/₂"

10¹/₂"

   - Cut 4 lengthwise strips 3" x 80" for **borders**.
   - Cut 4 **squares** 22" x 22" from fabric width left after cutting borders.
2. **From green:** ◼
   - Cut 3 squares 22" x 22".
3. **From red:** ◼
   - Cut 7 selvage-to-selvage **strips** 2¹/₂"w.
   - Cut 1 **square** 22" x 22".
4. **From yellow:** ◻
   - Cut 2 selvage-to-selvage **strips** 2¹/₂"w.

ASSEMBLING THE QUILT TOP

Follow **Piecing and Pressing**, *page 113, to assemble* **Qu Top**.

1. To make **triangle-squares**, place 1 white and 1 red **square** right sides together. Referring to **Fig. 1** follow Steps 1 - 3 of **Making Triangle-Squares**, page 114, to mark a grid of 49 squares 2⁷/₈" x 2⁷/₈ Referring to **Fig. 2** and starting and ending stitching as necessary, follow Steps 4 - 6 of **Making Triangle-squares**, page 114, to complete 98 **triangle-squares** (you will need 96 and have 2 left over).

Fig. 1

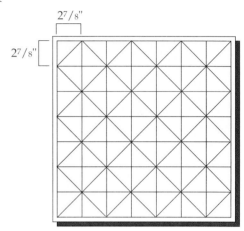

2⁷/₈"

2⁷/₈"

Fig. 2

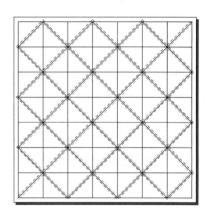

triangle-square (make 98)

2. Using white and green **squares**, repeat Step 1 to make a total of 294 **triangle-squares** (you will need 288 and have 6 left over).

triangle-square (make 294)

48

Assemble 4 **triangle-squares** as shown to make Unit 1. Make 96 **Unit 1's**.

Unit 1 (make 96)

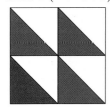

Assemble 2¹/₂"w **strips** as shown to make **Strip Set A**. Make 3 **Strip Set A's**. Cut across **Strip Set A's** at 2¹/₂" intervals to make a total of 48 **Unit 2's**.

Strip Set A (make 3)   **Unit 2** (make 48)

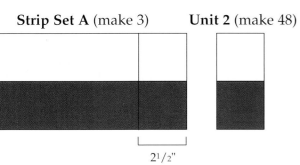

2¹/₂"

Assemble 2 **Unit 1's** and 1 **Unit 2** as shown to make **Unit 3**. Make 48 **Unit 3's**.

Unit 3 (make 48)

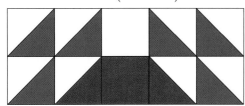

Assemble 2¹/₂"w **strips** as shown to make **Strip Set B**. Make 2 **Strip Set B's**. Cut across **Strip Set B's** at 2¹/₂" intervals to make a total of 24 **Unit 4's**.

Strip Set B (make 2)   **Unit 4** (make 24)

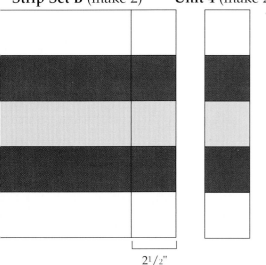

2¹/₂"

7. Assemble 2 **Unit 3's** and 1 **Unit 4** to make **Block**. Make 24 **Blocks**.

Block (make 24)

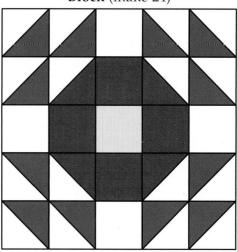

8. Assemble 4 **setting squares** and 3 **Blocks** as shown to make **Row A**. Make 4 **Row A's**.

Row A (make 4)

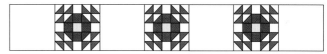

9. Assemble 4 **Blocks** and 3 **setting squares** as shown to make **Row B**. Make 3 **Row B's**.

Row B (make 3)

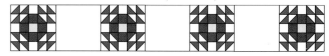

10. Referring to **Quilt Top Diagram**, page 50, assemble **Rows** to complete center section of **Quilt Top**.
11. Follow **Adding Mitered Borders**, page 119, and **Quilt Top Diagram**, page 50, to complete **Quilt Top**.

COMPLETING THE QUILT

1. Follow **Quilting**, page 119, **Quilting Diagram**, and **Quilting Patterns**, page 50, to mark, layer, and quilt. Our quilt is hand quilted.
2. Cut a 36" square of binding fabric. Follow **Making Continuous Bias Strip Binding**, page 123, to make approximately 9 yds of 2¹/₂"w bias binding.
3. Follow **Attaching Binding with Mitered Corners**, page 124, to attach binding to quilt.

Quilt Top Diagram

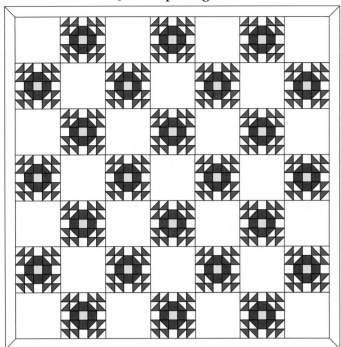

Quilting Pattern

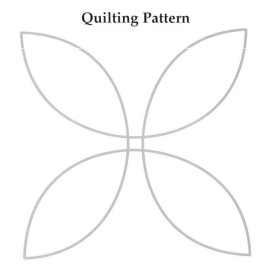

Quilting Diagram

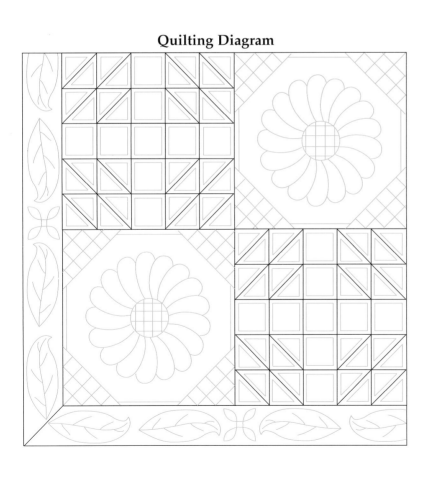

Quilting Pattern

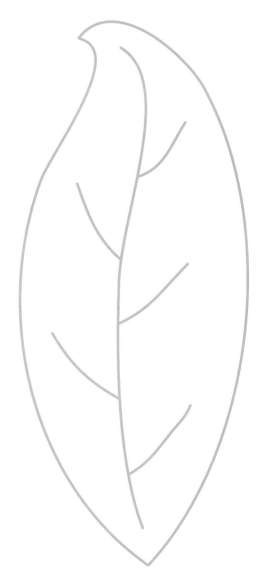

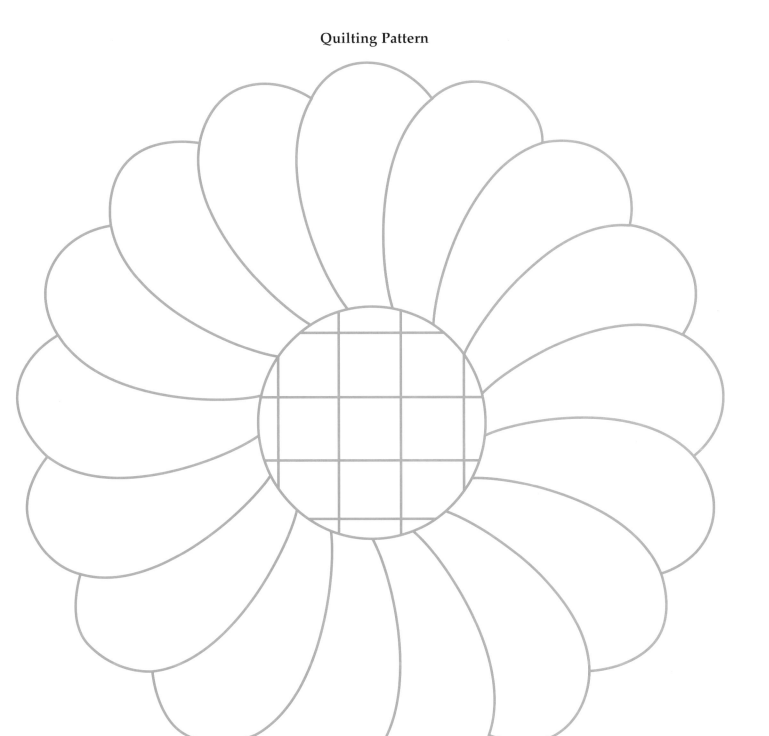

Garden
Wedding

An Irish Chain pattern forms the background
of this lovely quilt, but the sunny blossoms are
Nine-Patch blocks with easy appliqué leaves.
Hearts and hands celebrate a joyous union on
the matching wall hanging, page 58.

GARDEN WEDDING QUILT

SKILL LEVEL: 1 2 3 4 5
QUILT SIZE: 91" x 109"

YARDAGE REQUIREMENTS

Yardage is based on 45"w fabric.

☐ 6³/₈ yds of cream print

▨ 3¹/₄ yds of green print

▦ 2¹/₂ yds of pink print

☐ ³/₄ yd of yellow print
  8¹/₄ yds for backing
  1 yd for binding
  120" x 120" batting

You will also need:
  paper-backed fusible web
  transparent monofilament thread for appliqué

CUTTING OUT THE PIECES

All measurements include a ¹/₄" seam allowance. Follow
***Rotary Cutting**, page 110, to cut fabric unless otherwise*
indicated.

1. **From cream print:** ☐
    * Cut 53 **strips** 2¹/₂"w.
    * Cut 6 **wide strips** 3¹/₄"w.
    * Cut 5 strips 4¹/₂"w. From these strips,
      cut 40 **squares** 4¹/₂" x 4¹/₂".
    * Cut 5 strips 6¹/₂"w. From these strips,
      cut 25 **small rectangles** 2¹/₂" x 6¹/₂"
      and 24 **large rectangles** 4¹/₂" x 6¹/₂".

2. **From green print:** ▨
    * Cut 30 **strips** 2¹/₂"w.
    * Cut 3 **narrow** strips 1"w.
    * Cut 3 strips 4¹/₂"w. From these strips, cut 20
      squares 4¹/₂" x 4¹/₂".
    * Use pattern, page 60, and follow **Preparing
      Appliqué Pieces**, page 116, to make
      50 **leaf** appliqués.

3. **From pink print:** ▦
    * Cut 32 **strips** 2¹/₂"w.

4. **From yellow print:** ☐
    * Cut 8 **strips** 2¹/₂"w.

ASSEMBLING THE QUILT TOP

*Follow **Piecing and Pressing**, page 113, to make quilt top.*

1. Sew 3 **strips** together to make **Strip Set A**. Make 7
    Strip Set A's. Cut across **Strip Set A's** at 2¹/₂"
    intervals to make 104 **Unit 1's**.

Strip Set A (make 7)   **Unit 1** (make 104)

2¹/₂"

2. Sew 3 **strips** together to make **Strip Set B**. Make 3
    Strip Set B's. Cut across **Strip Set B's** at 2¹/₂"
    intervals to make 34 **Unit 2's**.

Strip Set B (make 3)   **Unit 2** (make 34)

2¹/₂"

3. Sew 3 **strips** together to make **Strip Set C**. Make 9
    Strip Set C's. Cut across 3 **Strip Set C's** at 2¹/₂"
    intervals to make 48 **Unit 3's**. Cut across 2 **Strip
    Set C's** at 4¹/₂" intervals to make 18 **Unit 4's**. Cut
    across remaining **Strip Set C's** at 6¹/₂" intervals to
    make 22 **Unit 5's**.

Strip Set C (make 9)   **Unit 3** (make 48)

2¹/₂"

Unit 4 (make 18)   **Unit 5** (make 22)

4¹/₂"   6¹/₂"

4. Sew 3 **strips** together to make **Strip Set D**. Make 3
    Strip Set D's. Cut across **Strip Set D's** at 2¹/₂"
    intervals to make 48 **Unit 6's**.

Strip Set D (make 3)   **Unit 6** (make 48)

2¹/₂"

54

5. Sew 2 **strips** together to make **Strip Set E**. Make 10 **Strip Set E's**. Cut across **Strip Set E's** at $2^1/2$" intervals to make 160 **Unit 7's**.

Strip Set E (make 10)   **Unit 7** (make 160)

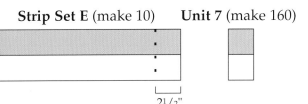

6. Sew 2 **strips** together to make **Strip Set F**. Make 5 **Strip Set F's**. Cut across **Strip Set F's** at $4^1/2$" intervals to make 40 **Unit 8's**.

Strip Set F (make 5)   **Unit 8** (make 40)

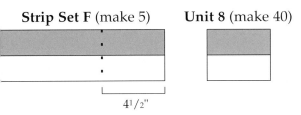

7. Sew 3 **strips** together to make **Strip Set G**. Make 4 **Strip Set G's**. Cut across **Strip Set G's** at $2^1/2$" intervals to make 50 **Unit 9's**.

Strip Set G (make 4)   **Unit 9** (make 50)

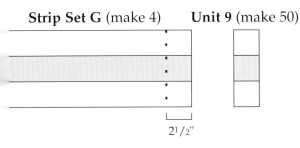

8. Sew 3 **strips** together to make **Strip Set H**. Make 2 **Strip Set H's**. Cut across **Strip Set H's** at $2^1/2$" intervals to make 25 **Unit 10's**.

Strip Set H (make 2)   **Unit 10** (make 25)

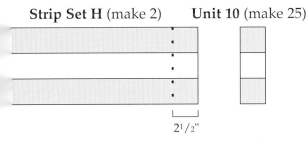

9. Sew 1 **narrow** and 2 **wide strips** together to make **Strip Set I**. Make 3 **Strip Set I's**. Cut across **Strip Set I's** at $4^1/2$" intervals to make 25 **Unit 11's**.

Strip Set I (make 3)   **Unit 11** (make 25)

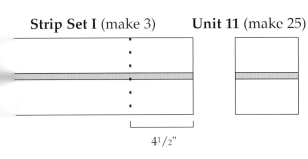

10. Sew 3 **strips** together to make **Strip Set J**. Make 3 **Strip Set J's**. Cut across **Strip Set J's** at $2^1/2$" intervals to make 36 **Unit 12's**.

Strip Set J (make 3)   **Unit 12** (make 36)

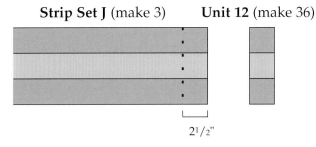

11. Sew 2 **Unit 1's** and 1 **Unit 2** together to make **Block A**. Make 34 **Block A's**.

Block A (make 34)

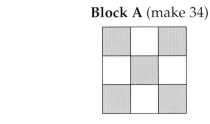

12. Sew 2 **Unit 3's**, 2 **Unit 6's**, and 1 **large rectangle** together to make **Block B**. Make 24 **Block B's**.

Block B (make 24)

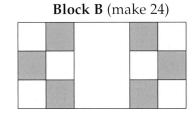

13. Sew 2 **Unit 7's** together to make **Unit 13**. Make 80 **Unit 13's**.

Unit 13 (make 80)

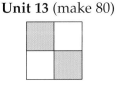

14. Sew 2 **Unit 13's** and 1 **Unit 8** together to make **Unit 14**. Make 40 **Unit 14's**.

Unit 14 (make 40)

55

15. Sew 3 **squares** together to make **Unit 15**. Make 20 **Unit 15's**.

Unit 15 (make 20)

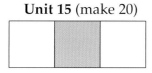

16. Sew 2 **Unit 14's** and 1 **Unit 15** together to make **Block C**. Make 20 **Block C's**.

Block C (make 20)

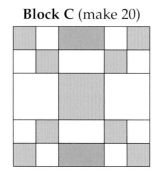

17. Sew 2 **Unit 9's** and 1 **Unit 10** together to make **Unit 16**. Make 25 **Unit 16's**.

Unit 16 (make 25)

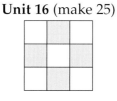

18. Sew 1 **small rectangle**, 1 **Unit 16**, and 1 **Unit 11** together to make **Unit 17**. Make 25 **Unit 17's**.

Unit 17 (make 25)

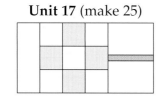

19. Follow **Invisible Appliqué**, page 116, to stitch 2 **leaf** appliqués to 1 **Unit 17** to make **Block D**. Make 25 **Block D's**.

Block D (make 25)

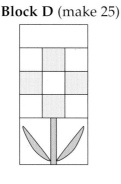

20. Sew 1 **Unit 1** and 1 **Unit 12** together to make **Unit 18**. Make 36 **Unit 18's**.

Unit 18 (make 36)

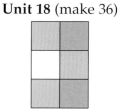

21. Sew 2 **Unit 18's** and 1 **Unit 4** together to make **Block E**. Make 18 **Block E's**.

Block E (make 18)

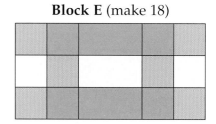

22. Sew 2 **Block A's**, 5 **Unit 5's**, and 4 **Block E's** together to make **Row A**. Make 2 **Row A's**.

Row A (make 2)

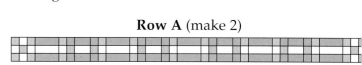

23. Sew 2 **Unit 5's**, 5 **Block A's**, and 4 **Block B's** together to make **Row B**. Make 6 **Row B's**.

Row B (make 6)

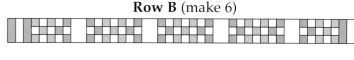

24. Sew 2 **Block E's**, 5 **Block D's**, and 4 **Block C's** together to make **Row C**. Make 5 **Row C's**.

Row C (make 5)

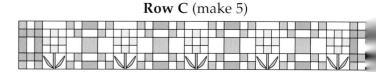

25. Referring to **Quilt Top Diagram**, page 57, sew **Rows** together to complete **Quilt Top**.

OMPLETING THE QUILT

Follow **Quilting**, page 119, to mark, layer, and quilt using **Quilting Diagram**, as a suggestion. Our quilt is hand quilted.

Cut a 34" square of binding fabric. Follow **Binding**, page 123, to bind quilt using $2^1/_2$"w bias binding with mitered corners.

Quilting Diagram

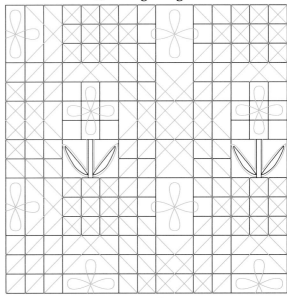

Quilt Top Diagram

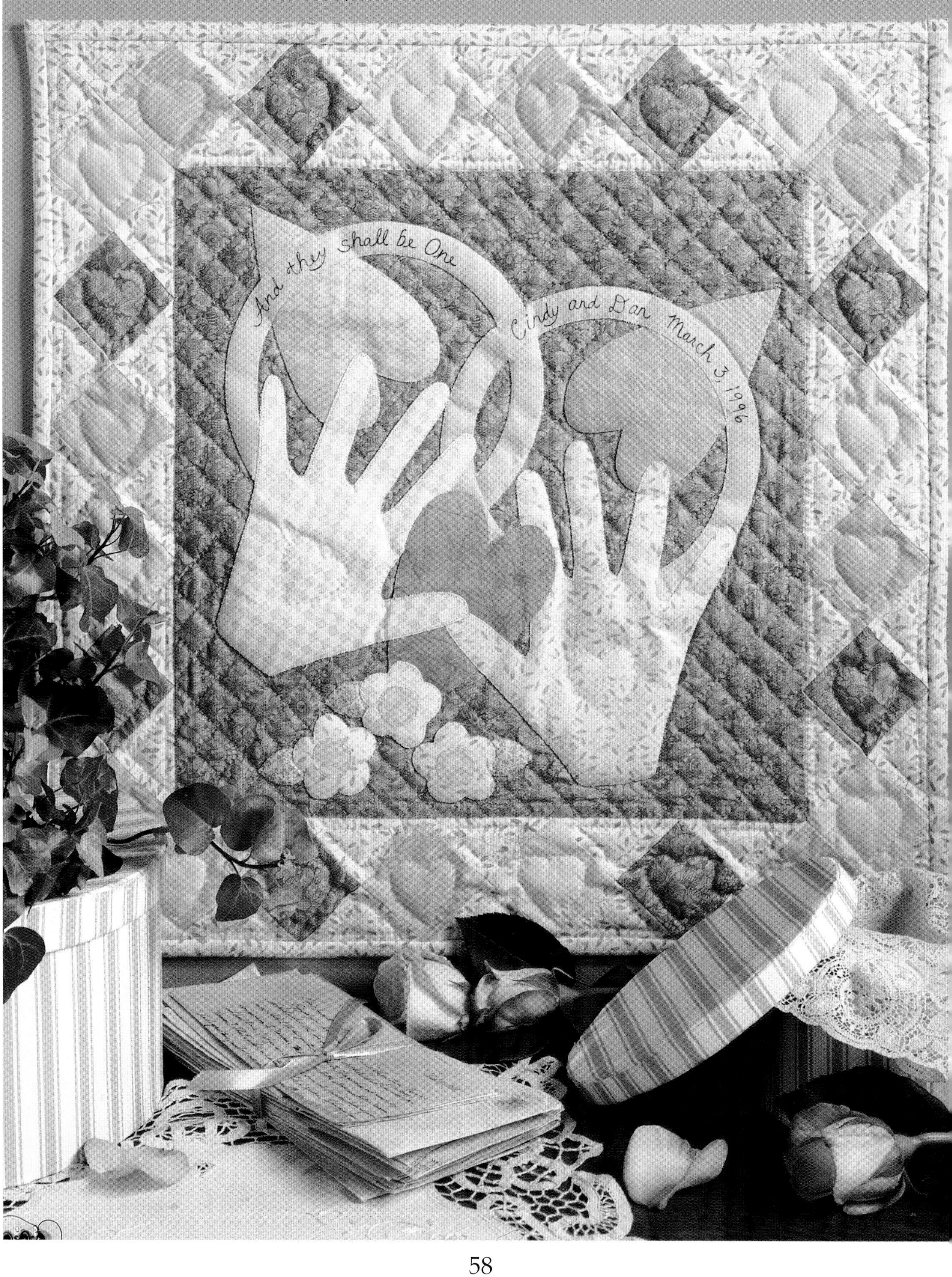
And they shall be One
Cindy and Dan March 3, 1996

ARDEN WEDDING WALL HANGING

KILL LEVEL: 1 2 3 4 5
ALL HANGING SIZE: 22" x 22"

ARDAGE REQUIREMENTS

rdage is based on 45"w fabric.

- 1/2 yd of green print
- 3/8 yd of cream print
- 1/8 yd of pink print
- 1/8 yd of yellow solid
- scraps of assorted prints for appliqués
- 3/4 yd for backing and hanging sleeve
- 3/8 yd for binding
- 25" x 25" batting

u will also need:
- paper-backed fusible web
- transparent monofilament thread for appliqué
- black permanent fabric pen

UTTING OUT THE PIECES

*measurements include a 1/4" seam allowance. Follow
tary Cutting, page 110, to cut fabric unless otherwise
dicated.*

From green print:
- Cut 1 **background** 16" x 16".
- Cut 8 **squares** 2⅝" x 2⅝".

From cream print: ☐
- Cut 2 strips 4¼"w. From these strips, cut 12 squares 4¼" x 4¼". Cut squares twice diagonally to make 48 **triangles**.

From pink print: ■
- Cut 1 strip 2⅝"w. From this strip, cut 8 **squares** 2⅝" x 2⅝".

From yellow solid: ☐
- Cut 1 strip 2⅝"w. From this strip, cut 8 **squares** 2⅝" x 2⅝".

From remaining fabric and scraps: ◨
- Referring to photo, use patterns, pages 60-61, and follow **Preparing Appliqué Pieces**, page 116, to make the following **appliqués**:
  - 2 **hands** (1 in reverse) 3 **flowers**
  - 3 **hearts** 3 **flower centers**
  - 2 **rings** 3 **small leaves**

ASSEMBLING THE WALL HANGING TOP

*Refer to photo and **Wall Hanging Top Diagram**, page 60, and follow **Piecing and Pressing**, page 113, to make wall hanging top.*

1. Use fabric marking pen to write words on **rings**.
2. Follow **Invisible Appliqué**, page 116, to stitch **pieces** to **background**. Trim **background** to measure 15½" x 15½".
3. Use **triangles** and **squares** to make 4 **Unit 1's**, 8 **Unit 2's**, 8 **Unit 3's**, and 4 **Unit 4's**.

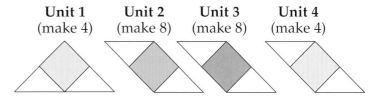

| Unit 1 (make 4) | Unit 2 (make 8) | Unit 3 (make 8) | Unit 4 (make 4) |

4. Sew 1 **Unit 1**, 2 **Unit 2's**, 2 **Unit 3's**, and 1 **Unit 4** together to make **Border Unit**. Make 4 **Border Units**.

Border Unit (make 4)

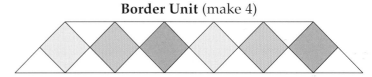

5. Beginning and ending stitching exactly 1/4" from each corner of background and backstitching at beginning and end of each seam, sew 1 **Border Unit** to each edge of **background**.
6. Fold 1 corner of wall hanging top diagonally with right sides together, matching outer edges of borders. Beginning at point where previous seams ended, stitch corner seam (**Fig. 1**) to complete **Wall Hanging Top**.

Fig. 1

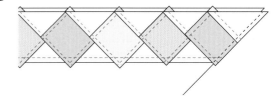

COMPLETING THE WALL HANGING

1. Follow **Quilting**, page 119, to mark, layer, and quilt, using **Quilting Diagram** as a suggestion. Our wall hanging is hand quilted.
2. Follow **Making a Hanging Sleeve**, page 125, to attach hanging sleeve.
3. Follow **Binding**, page 123, to bind quilt using 2¹/₂"w straight-grain binding with overlapped corners.

Quilting Diagram

Wall Hanging Top Diagram

Small Leaf

Flower

Flower Center

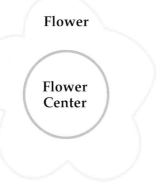

Leaf

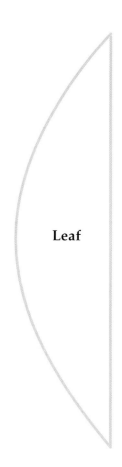

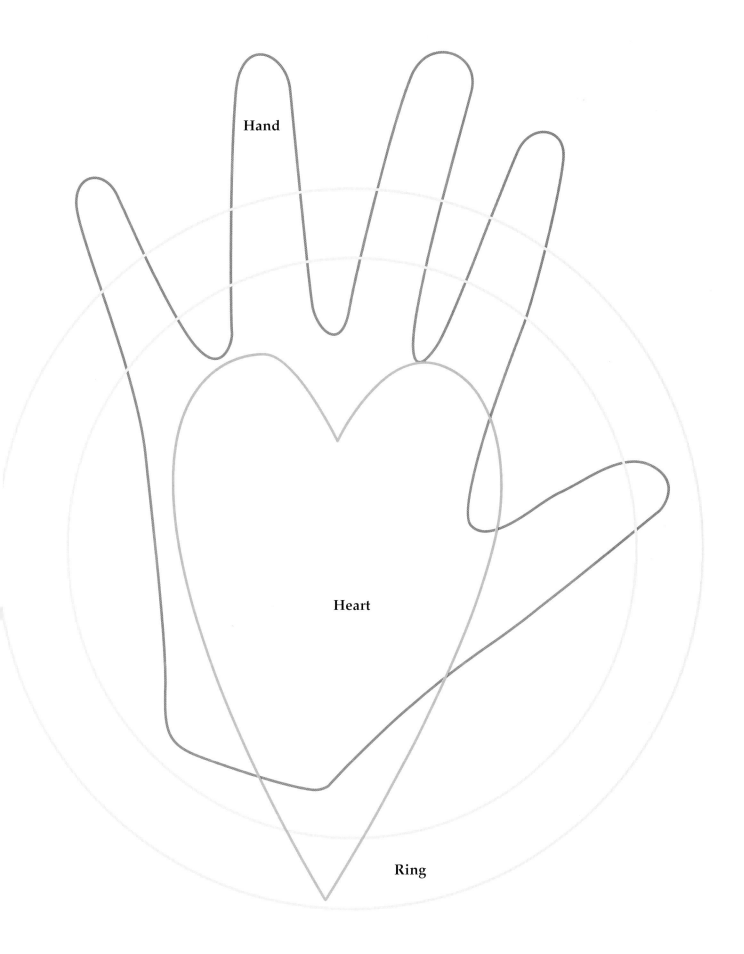

Hand

Heart

Ring

Stylish
Cake Stand

A graceful display for baked delights, the time-honored cake stand has served for generations as the centerpiece for home-style celebrations. Triangle-squares and a quick grid technique make the Cake Stand pattern easy. The matching wall hanging on page 67 blossoms with appliqué and buttons!

STYLISH CAKE STAND QUILT

SKILL LEVEL: 1 2 3 4 5
BLOCK SIZE: 7¹/₂" x 7¹/₂"
QUILT SIZE: 79" x 89"

YARDAGE REQUIREMENTS
Yardage is based on 45"w fabric.

- 4¹/₂ yds of blue solid
- 4 yds of white solid
- 2¹/₂ yds of light blue solid
- 7¹/₄ yds for backing
- 1 yd for binding
- 90" x 108" batting

CUTTING OUT THE PIECES
All measurements include a ¹/₄" seam allowance. Follow **Rotary Cutting**, *page 110, to cut fabric.*

1. **From blue solid:**
   - Cut 2 lengthwise **side outer borders** 5¹/₂" x 93".
   - Cut 2 lengthwise **top/bottom outer borders** 5¹/₂" x 72".
   - Cut 2 **large rectangles** 18" x 23" for large triangle-squares.
   - Cut 4 **rectangles** 16" x 18" for small triangle-squares.
   - Cut 4 strips 5"w. From these strips, cut 84 **small rectangles** 2" x 5".
   - Cut 4 strips 2"w. From these strips, cut 84 **small squares** 2" x 2".

2. **From white solid:**
   - Cut 2 **large rectangles** 18" x 23" for large triangle-squares.
   - Cut 4 **rectangles** 16" x 18" for small triangle-squares.
   - Cut 6 strips 8"w. From these strips, cut 30 **setting squares** 8" x 8".
   - Cut 6 squares 11⁷/₈" x 11⁷/₈". Cut squares twice diagonally to make 24 **side triangles**. (You will need 22 and have 2 left over.)
   - Cut 2 squares 6¹/₄" x 6¹/₄". Cut squares once diagonally to make 4 **corner triangles**.

3. **From light blue solid:**
   - Cut 2 lengthwise **side inner borders** 2¹/₂" x 83".
   - Cut 2 lengthwise **top/bottom inner borders** 2¹/₂" x 68".

ASSEMBLING THE QUILT TOP
Follow **Piecing and Pressing**, *page 113, to make quilt top.*

1. To make small triangle-squares, place 1 blue and 1 white **rectangle** right sides together. Referring to **Fig. 1**, follow **Making Triangle-Squares**, page 114, to make 84 **small triangle-squares**. Repeat with remaining **rectangles** to make a total of 336 **small triangle-squares**.

Fig. 1

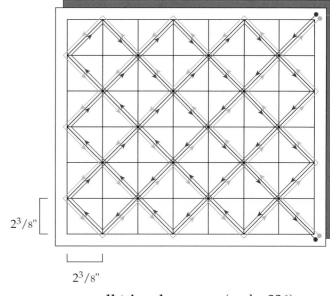

2³/₈"

2³/₈"

small triangle-square (make 336)

2. To make large triangle-squares, place 1 blue and white **large rectangle** right sides together. Referring to **Fig. 2**, follow **Making Triangle-Squares**, page 114, to make 24 **large triangle-squares**. Repeat with remaining **large rectangles** to make a total of 48 **large triangle-squares**. (You will need 42 and have 6 left over.)

Fig. 2

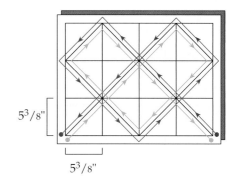

5³/₈"

5³/₈"

large triangle-square (make 48)

3. Sew 3 **small triangle-squares** together to make **Unit 1**. Make 42 **Unit 1's**.

Unit 1 (make 42)

64

4. Sew 3 **small triangle-squares** and one **small square** together to make **Unit 2**. Make 42 **Unit 2's**.

Unit 2 (make 42)

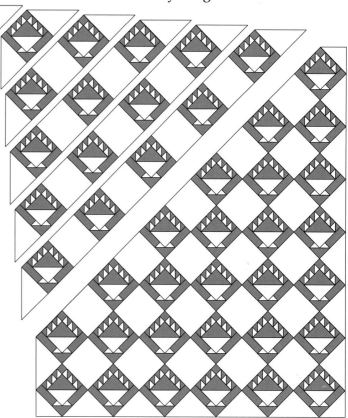

5. Sew 1 **large triangle-square**, 1 **Unit 1**, and 1 **Unit 2** together to make **Unit 3**. Make 42 **Unit 3's**.

Unit 3 (make 42)

6. Sew 1 **small rectangle** and 1 **small triangle-square** together to make **Unit 4**. Make 42 **Unit 4's**.

Unit 4 (make 42)

7. Sew 1 **small square**, 1 **small triangle-square**, and 1 **small rectangle** together to make **Unit 5**. Make 42 **Unit 5's**.

Unit 5 (make 42)

Quilt Top Diagram

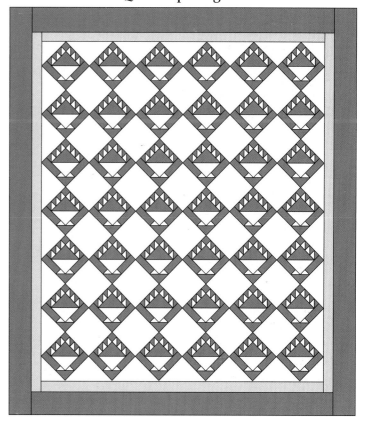

8. Sew 1 **Unit 3**, 1 **Unit 4**, then 1 **Unit 5** together to make **Block**. Make 42 **Blocks**.

Block (make 42)

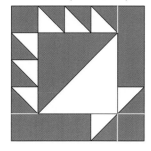

Referring to **Assembly Diagram**, sew **corner triangles**, **side triangles**, **setting squares**, and **Blocks** together into diagonal rows. Sew rows together to make center section of quilt top.

9. Follow **Adding Squared Borders**, page 118, to add **top**, **bottom**, then **side inner borders** to center section. Repeat to add **outer borders** to complete quilt top.

COMPLETING THE QUILT

1. Follow **Quilting**, page 119, to mark, layer, and quilt, using **Quilting Diagram** as a suggestion. Our quilt is hand quilted.
2. Cut a 32" square of binding fabric. Follow **Binding**, page 123, to bind quilt using 2¹/₂"w bias binding with mitered corners.

Quilting Diagram

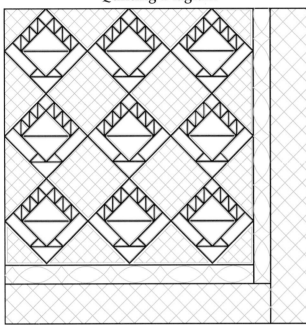

STYLISH CAKE STAND WALL HANGING

SKILL LEVEL: 1 2 3 4 5
WALL HANGING SIZE: 30" x 30"

YARDAGE REQUIREMENTS

Yardage is based on 45"w fabric.

☐ 1¹/₄ yd of white solid
▣ ³/₈ yd of blue solid
▣ ³/₈ yd of light blue print
▣ ¹/₄ yd of blue print
▣ ¹/₄ yd of dark blue print
▣ scraps of light blue solid and blue check for appliqués
  1 yd for backing and hanging sleeve
  ⁵/₈ yd for binding
  32" x 32" batting

You will also need:
  paper-backed fusible web
  transparent monofilament thread
  25 blue ¹/₄" dia. buttons

CUTTING OUT THE PIECES

All measurements include a ¹/₄" seam allowance. Follow Rotary Cutting, page 110, to cut fabric.

1. **From white solid:** ☐
   - Cut 1 **square** 6" x 6" for triangle-squares.
   - Cut 1 square 5³/₈" x 5³/₈". Cut square once diagonally to make 2 **triangles**. (You will need ? and have 1 left over.)
   - Cut 4 **large rectangles** 3³/₄" x 8".
   - Cut 4 **square B's** 3³/₄" x 3³/₄".
   - Cut 4 squares 6³/₈" x 6³/₈". Cut squares once diagonally to make 8 **large triangles**.
   - Cut 7 **strips** 1¹/₂" x 7".
   - Cut 2 **square C's** 1¹/₂" x 1¹/₂".
   - Cut 4 **square D's** 3¹/₄" x 3¹/₄".
   - Cut 16 **small rectangles** 3¹/₄" x 1⁷/₈".
   - Cut 16 **small square D's** 1⁷/₈" x 1⁷/₈".
   - Cut 2 squares 3⁵/₈" x 3⁵/₈". Cut squares once diagonally to make 4 **large border triangles**.
   - Cut 8 squares 4" x 4". Cut squares twice diagonally to make 32 **small border triangles**.

2. **From blue solid:** ▣
   - Cut 7 **strips** 1¹/₂" x 7".
   - Cut 2 **square C's** 1¹/₂" x 1¹/₂".
   - Cut 8 squares 3⁵/₈" x 3⁵/₈". Cut squares once diagonally to make 16 **large border triangles**.
   - Cut 4 squares 4" x 4". Cut squares twice diagonally to make 16 **small border triangles**.

3. **From light blue print:** ▣
   - Cut 32 **small square D's** 1⁷/₈" x 1⁷/₈".
   - Cut 10 squares 3⁵/₈" x 3⁵/₈". Cut squares once diagonally to make 20 **large border triangles**.
   - Cut 4 squares 4" x 4". Cut squares twice diagonally to make 16 **small border triangles**.

4. **From blue print:** ▣
   - Cut 1 **square** 6" x 6" for triangles-squares.
   - Cut 1 square 5³/₈" x 5³/₈". Cut square once diagonally to make 2 **triangles**. (You will need 1 and have 1 left over.)
   - Cut 2 **small square A's** 2" x 2".
   - Cut 2 **small rectangles** 2" x 5".

5. **From dark blue print:** ▣
   - Cut 2 **top/bottom borders** 1¹/₄" x 29¹/₂".
   - Cut 2 **side borders** 1¹/₄" x 28".

6. **From remaining fabric and scraps:** ▣
   - Using patterns, page 71, and referring to **Wall Hanging Top Diagram**, page 70, follow **Preparing Appliqué Pieces**, page 116, to make the following appliqués:

1 **flower**	2 **leaf**
1 **flower center**	2 **bud A**
1 **stem A**	4 **bud B**
1 **stem B**	4 **bud C**
4 **stem C**	

67

ASSEMBLING THE WALL HANGING TOP

*Follow **Piecing and Pressing**, page 113, to make wall hanging top.*

1. To make triangle-squares, place white and blue print **squares** right sides together. Referring to **Fig. 1**, follow **Making Triangle-Squares**, page 114, to make 8 **triangle-squares**.

Fig. 1

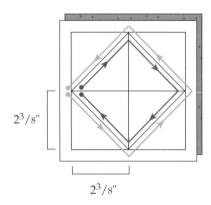

$2^3/8"$

$2^3/8"$

triangle-square (make 8)

2. Sew 3 **triangle-squares** together to make **Unit 1**.

Unit 1

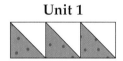

3. Sew 3 **triangle-squares** and 1 **small square A** together to make **Unit 2**.

Unit 2

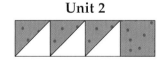

4. Sew 2 **triangles** together to make **Unit 3**.

Unit 3

5. Sew 1 **small rectangle** and 1 **triangle-square** together to make **Unit 4**.

Unit 4

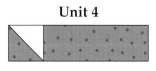

6. Sew 1 **small rectangle**, 1 **triangle-square**, and 1 **small square A** together to make **Unit 5**.

Unit 5

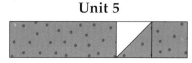

7. Referring to **Cake Stand Block** diagram, sew **Units 1 - 5** together to make **Cake Stand Block**.

Cake Stand Block

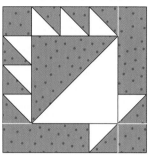

8. Sew 1 **large rectangle** each to top and bottom edge of **Cake Stand Block**. Sew 1 **square B** to each end of each remaining **large rectangle**. Sew rectangles to side edges of **Cake Stand Block** to make **Unit 6**.

Unit 6

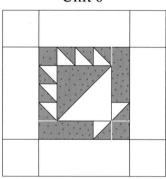

9. Sew **strips** together to make **Strip Set**. Cut across **Strip Set** at $1^1/2"$ intervals to make 4 **Unit 7's**.

Strip Set   **Unit 7** (make 4)

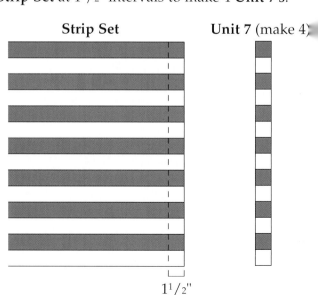

$1^1/2"$

68

0. Sew 1 **Unit 7** each to top and bottom edges of **Unit 6**. Sew **square C's** to each end of each remaining **Unit 7**. Sew **Unit 7's** to side edges of **Unit 6** to make **Unit 8**.

Unit 8

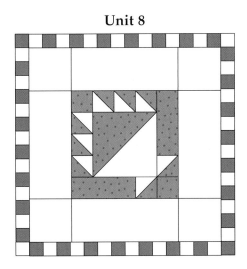

1. Place 1 **small square D** on 1 **small rectangle** and stitch diagonally (**Fig. 2**). Trim ¹/₄" from stitching (**Fig. 3**). Press open, pressing seam allowance toward darker fabric.

ig. 2

Fig. 3

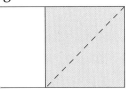

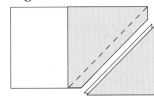

2. Place 1 **small square D** on opposite end of **small rectangle** and stitch diagonally (**Fig. 4**). Trim ¹/₄" from stitching (**Fig. 5**). Press open, pressing seam allowance toward darker fabric, to make **Unit 9**.

ig. 4

Fig. 5

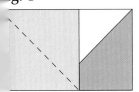

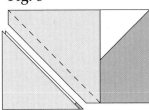

Unit 9

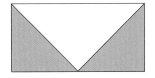

13. Repeat Steps 11 and 12 to make 16 **Unit 9's**.

14. Sew 1 **Unit 9** and 2 **small square D's** together to make **Unit 10**. Make 8 **Unit 10's**.

Unit 10 (make 8)

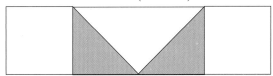

15. Sew 2 **Unit 9's** and 1 **square D** together to make **Unit 11**. Make 4 **Unit 11's**.

Unit 11 (make 4)

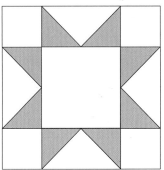

16. Sew 2 **Unit 10's** and 1 **Unit 11** together to make **Variable Star Block**. Make 4 **Variable Star Blocks**.

Variable Star Block (make 4)

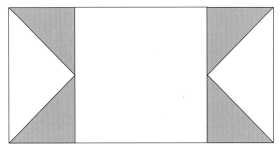

17. Sew 1 **Variable Star Block** and 2 **large triangles** together to make **Unit 12**. Make 4 **Unit 12's**.

Unit 12 (make 4)

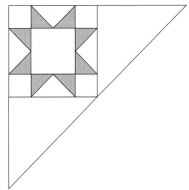

18. Referring to **Wall Hanging Top Diagram**, sew **Unit 8** and **Unit 12's** together to make center section of wall hanging top.
19. Sew 2 **large border triangles** together to make **Unit 13**. Make 4 **Unit 13's**.

Unit 13 (make 4)

20. Referring to diagrams for color placement, use **large border triangles** and **small border triangles** to make 8 *each* of **Units 14 - 17**.

Unit 14 (make 8)

Unit 15 (make 8)

Unit 16 (make 8)

Unit 17 (make 8)

21. Using 2 *each* of **Units 14 - 17** and referring to diagram for placement, sew units together to make **Ribbon Border Unit**. Make 4 **Ribbon Border Units**.

Ribbon Border Unit (make 4)

22. Sew 1 **Ribbon Border Unit** to each side edge of center section. Sew 1 **Unit 13** to each end of each remaining **Ribbon Border Unit**. Sew **Ribbon Border Units** to top and bottom edges of center section.
23. Sew **side**, then **top** and **bottom outer borders** to center section.
24. Referring to **Wall Hanging Top Diagram**, arrange **appliqués** on **Cake Stand Block** and **Variable Star Blocks**, overlapping as necessary; fuse in place. Follow **Invisible Appliqué**, page 116, to stitch appliqués in place to complete **Wall Hanging Top**.

COMPLETING THE WALL HANGING
1. Follow **Quilting**, page 119, to mark, layer, and quilt wall hanging, using **Quilting Diagram** as a suggestion. Our wall hanging is hand quilted.
2. Follow **Making a Hanging Sleeve**, page 125, to attach hanging sleeve to wall hanging.
3. Cut a 20" square of binding fabric. Follow **Binding**, page 123, to bind wall hanging using $2^1/2$"w bias binding with mitered corners.
4. Referring to **Wall Hanging Top Diagram**, sew buttons to front of wall hanging.

Quilting Diagram

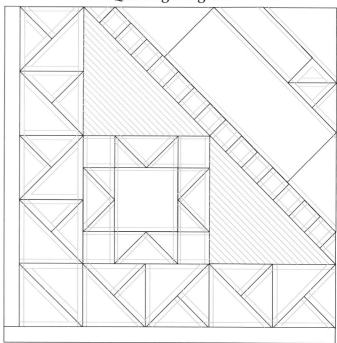

Wall Hanging Top Diagram

70

Flower

Stem
A

Bud
C

Bud
A

Flower
Center

Stem
B

Bud
B

Leaf

Stem
C

Spring
Bouquet

Most people won't notice at first glance, but this floral print quilt has a secret. The pieces for the easy blocks were cut and sewn without any curves — it's the rounded quilting pattern that fools the eye! A coordinating tabletopper, pillows, and topiary wall hanging continue the romantic look.

SPRING BOUQUET QUILT

SKILL LEVEL: 1 2 3 4 5
BLOCK SIZE: 12" x 12"
QUILT SIZE: 85" x 97"

YARDAGE REQUIREMENTS
Yardage is based on 45"w fabric.

- $5^1/4$ yds of large floral print
- $3^5/8$ yds of small floral print
- $1^3/4$ yds of white print
- $1^3/4$ yds of green print
  $7^3/4$ yds for backing
  1 yd for binding
  120" x 120" batting

You will also need:
  Companion Angle™ Rotary Cutting Ruler (made
  by EZ International)

CUTTING OUT THE PIECES
All measurements include a $1/4$" seam allowance. Follow
Rotary Cutting, page 110, to cut fabric.

1. **From large floral print:**
   - Cut 8 selvage-to-selvage strips 9"w. From
     these strips, cut 32 **squares** 9" x 9".
   - Cut 2 lengthwise strips $6^1/2$" x 100" for
     side borders.
   - Cut 2 lengthwise strips $6^1/2$" x 76" for
     top/bottom borders.
   - From remaining fabric, cut 10 additional
     squares 9" x 9".
2. **From small floral print:**
   - Cut 42 selvage-to-selvage **strips** $2^3/4$"w.
3. **From white print:**
   - Cut 21 selvage-to-selvage **strips** $2^1/2$"w.
4. **From green print:**
   - Cut 21 selvage-to-selvage **strips** $2^1/2$"w.

ASSEMBLING THE QUILT TOP
Follow Piecing and Pressing, page 113, to make quilt top.

1. Assemble **strips** to make 21 **Strip Set A's** and 21
   Strip Set B's.

Strip Set A (make 21)   **Strip Set B** (make 21)

2. Line up 9" sewing line (dashed line) on
   Companion Angle™ ruler ($4^3/4$" from top of ruler)
   with bottom edge of **Strip Set A** (**Fig. 1**). Cut on
   both sides of ruler to make **Unit 1**. Make 84 **Unit
   1's**. Repeat with **Strip Set B's** to make 84 **Unit 2's**.

Fig. 1

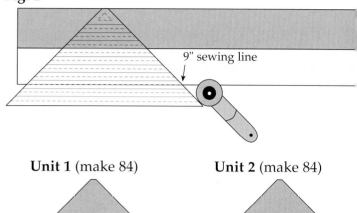

9" sewing line

Unit 1 (make 84)   **Unit 2** (make 84)

3. Assemble 4 **Unit 1's** and 1 **square** to make
   Block A. Make 21 **Block A's**. Assemble 4 **Unit 2's**
   and 1 **square** to make **Block B**. Make 21 **Block B's**

Block A (make 21)

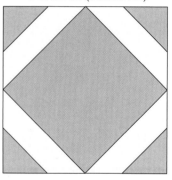

Block B (make 21)

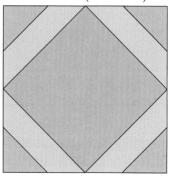

74

4. Assemble 3 **Block A's** and 3 **Block B's** to make **Row**. Make 7 **Rows**.

Row (make 7)

5. Referring to **Quilt Top Diagram**, assemble **Rows** to make center section of quilt top.
6. Follow **Adding Squared Borders**, page 118, to attach **top**, **bottom**, then **side borders** to center section to complete **Quilt Top**.

COMPLETING THE QUILT

1. Follow **Quilting**, page 119, to mark, layer, and quilt, using **Quilting Diagram** as a suggestion. Our quilt is hand quilted using **Quilting Pattern**, page 83.
2. Cut a 32" square of binding fabric. Follow **Binding**, page 123, to bind quilt using $2^1/2$"w bias binding with mitered corners.

Quilting Diagram

Quilt Top Diagram

BOUQUET BLOCK PILLOW

PILLOW SIZE: 12^{1}/$_{2}$" x 12^{1}/$_{2}$"

SUPPLIES
Yardage is based on 45"w fabric.

^{1}/$_{8}$ yd of small floral print
^{1}/$_{8}$ yd of green print
9" x 9" square of large floral print
16" x 16" pillow top backing
12^{1}/$_{2}$" x 12^{1}/$_{2}$" pillow back
^{1}/$_{4}$ yd for binding
16" x 16" batting
polyester fiberfill
Companion Angle™ Rotary Cutting Ruler (made
   by EZ International)

MAKING THE PILLOW
All measurements include a ^{1}/$_{4}$" seam allowance. Follow Rotary Cutting, page 110, to cut fabric. Follow Piecing and Pressing, page 113, to make pillow.

1. Cut 1 selvage-to-selvage strip 2^{1}/$_{2}$"w from green print and 1 selvage-to-selvage strip 2^{3}/$_{4}$"w from small floral print.

2. Using strips and 9" x 9" square, refer to Steps 1 - 3 of **Assembling the Quilt Top** for **Spring Bouquet Quilt**, page 74, to make 1 **Block B**.

3. Follow Step 1 of **Completing the Quilt** for **Spring Bouquet Quilt**, page 75, to quilt pillow top; trim backing and batting even with pillow top edges.

4. Place pillow back and pillow top wrong sides together. Sew pieces together, leaving an opening for stuffing.

5. Stuff pillow with fiberfill and sew opening closed.

6. From binding fabric, cut a 2" x 54" strip, pieced as necessary. Press strip in half lengthwise with wrong sides together. Follow **Attaching Binding with Mitered Corners**, page 124, to bind pillow.

ANDED ROLL PILLOW

ILLOW SIZE: 6" x 29$^1/_2$"

UPPLIES

$^5/_8$ yd of green print for pillow
scraps of assorted floral prints for pieced band
$^1/_4$ yd for pieced band backing
$^1/_4$ yd for binding
1$^3/_4$ yds of 2$^1/_2$"w wire-edge ribbon
2 strong rubber bands
polyester fiberfill

MAKING THE PILLOW

ll measurements include a $^1/_4$" seam allowance.
ollow Rotary Cutting, page 110, to cut fabric.
ollow Piecing and Pressing, page 113, to make pillow.

From floral print scraps, cut a total of 30 squares 2$^1/_2$" x 2$^1/_2$". Assemble squares to make pieced band.

pieced band

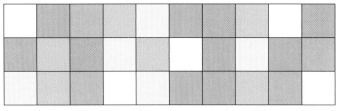

Cut pieced band backing 6$^1/_2$" x 20$^1/_2$". Place pieced band and pieced band backing wrong sides together and baste along long edges. From binding fabric, cut 2 strips 2" x 24"; press strips in half lengthwise with wrong sides together. Matching raw edges, sew 1 binding strip to front of pieced band along each long edge. Fold binding over to band backing and blindstitch in place. Trim ends of binding even with short ends of pieced band.

Sew short ends of pieced band together and turn right side out to complete pieced band.

For pillow, cut green print fabric 20" x 40". Press each short edge $^1/_4$" to wrong side; press 5" to wrong side again and stitch in place. Sew long edges together to form a tube. Turn right side out and press.

Wrap 1 rubber band around tube 5" from 1 end. Stuff tube with fiberfill and wrap remaining rubber band around tube 5" from remaining end.

Slip pieced band over pillow, centering band and matching seams; tack in place.

Cut ribbon in half. Tie 1 ribbon length into a bow around each end of pillow, covering rubber bands; trim ribbon ends.

FLORAL ENVELOPE PILLOW

PILLOW SIZE: 12$^1/_2$" x 18$^1/_2$"

SUPPLIES

$^3/_4$ yd of large floral print for pillow front
$^3/_4$ yd of small floral print for pillow back and flap
polyester fiberfill
nosegay of artificial flowers trimmed with
desired ribbons

MAKING THE PILLOW

All measurements include a $^1/_4$" seam allowance. Follow Rotary Cutting, page 110, to cut fabric. Follow Piecing and Pressing, page 113, to make pillow.

1. From large floral print, cut 1 pillow front 13$^3/_4$" x 19". For binding, cut 1 strip 2$^1/_2$" x 36" from remaining fabric; press strip in half lengthwise with wrong sides together.
2. From small floral print, cut 1 pillow back 19" x 21". For flap on pillow back fabric piece, refer to **Fig. 1** and cut a point at 1 short edge (top).

Fig. 1

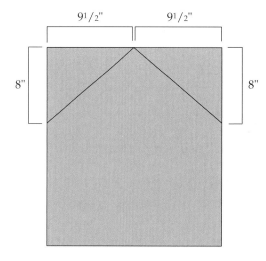

3. To bind flap on pillow back, follow **Attaching Binding with Mitered Corners**, page 124, mitering binding at point. Trim binding ends even with pillow back side edges.
4. Press 1 long edge (top) of pillow front $^1/_4$" to wrong side and stitch in place.
5. Matching side and bottom edges, place pillow front and pillow back right sides together and stitch side and bottom edges. Clip corners, turn right side out, and press.
6. Stuff pillow lightly with fiberfill. Blindstitch point of flap in place and add nosegay to complete pillow.

EDSIDE TABLE TOPPER

LOCK SIZE: 12" x 12"
ABLE TOPPER SIZE: 50" x 50"

ARDAGE REQUIREMENTS

rdage is based on 45"w fabric.

- [ ] $1^7/_8$ yds of large floral print
- [ ] $^7/_8$ yd of small floral print
- [ ] $^1/_2$ yd of green print
- [ ] $^3/_8$ yd of white print
  $3^1/_4$ yds for backing
  $^7/_8$ yd for binding
  72" x 90" batting

u will also need:
  Companion Angle™ Rotary Cutting Ruler
  (made by EZ International)

UTTING OUT THE PIECES

l measurements include a $^1/_4$" seam allowance. Follow
tary Cutting, page 110, to cut fabric.

From large floral print: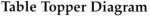

- Cut 1 selvage-to-selvage strip 9"w. From this strip, cut 4 **squares** 9" x 9".
- Cut 2 lengthwise strips $7^1/_2$" x $50^1/_2$" for **long borders**.
- Cut 2 lengthwise strips $7^1/_2$" x $36^1/_2$" for **short borders**.
- From remaining fabric, cut 5 additional **squares** 9" x 9".

From small floral print:

- Cut 9 selvage-to-selvage **strips** $2^3/_4$"w.

From green print:

- Cut 5 selvage-to-selvage **strips** $2^1/_2$"w.

From white print:

- Cut 4 selvage-to-selvage **strips** $2^1/_2$"w.

SSEMBLING THE TABLE TOPPER

llow Piecing and Pressing, page 113, to make table topper.

Assemble **strips** to make 4 **Strip Set A's** and 5 **Strip Set B's**.

rip Set A (make 4)

Strip Set B (make 5)

---

2. Follow Steps 2 and 3 of **Assembling the Quilt Top** for **Spring Bouquet Quilt**, page 74, to make 4 **Block A's** and 5 **Block B's**. (You will need 16 **Unit 1's** and 20 **Unit 2's** to make Blocks.)
3. Referring to **Table Topper Diagram**, assemble **Block A's** and **Block B's** to make center section of table topper.
4. Attach **short**, then **long border**s to center section to complete **Table Topper**.

COMPLETING THE TABLE TOPPER

1. Follow **Quilting**, page 119, to mark, layer, and quilt, using **Quilting Diagram**, page 75, as a suggestion. Our table topper is hand quilted using **Quilting Pattern**, page 83.
2. Cut a 26" square of binding fabric. Follow **Binding**, page 123, to bind table topper using $2^1/_2$"w bias binding with mitered corners.

Table Topper Diagram

TOPIARY WALL HANGING

KILL LEVEL: 1 2 3 4 5
WALL HANGING SIZE: 20" x 31"

YARDAGE REQUIREMENTS

Yardage is based on 45"w fabric.

- 1/2 yd of green print
- 3/8 yd of dark green print
- 1/8 yd of floral print for inner borders
- assorted floral print scraps for topiary, leaves, and stem
- light, medium, and dark tan print fabric scraps for basket
- 7/8 yd for backing and hanging sleeve
- 3/8 yd for binding
- 24" x 35" batting

You will also need:
- paper-backed fusible web
- fabric glue

CUTTING OUT THE PIECES

All measurements include a 1/4" seam allowance. Follow Rotary Cutting, page 110, to cut fabric unless otherwise indicated.

From green print: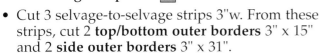

- Cut 1 **background** 13¹/₂" x 24¹/₂".

From dark green print:

- Cut 3 selvage-to-selvage strips 3"w. From these strips, cut 2 **top/bottom outer borders** 3" x 15" and 2 **side outer borders** 3" x 31".

From floral print for inner borders :

- Cut 2 selvage-to-selvage strips 1¹/₄"w. From these strips, cut 2 **top/bottom inner borders** 1¹/₄" x 15" and 2 **side inner borders** 1¹/₄" x 24¹/₂".

From assorted floral print scraps and tan print scraps:

- For topiary, cut a total of 25 floral print **squares** 2¹/₂" x 2¹/₂".
- For leaves, fuse web to wrong side(s) of desired floral print(s) and cut desired **leaf shapes** from fabric(s).
- For stem, fuse web to wrong side of one floral print and cut **stem** ³/₄" x 7¹/₄".
- For basket, use patterns, page 84, and follow **Preparing Appliqué Pieces**, page 116, to cut 1 **basket center** from light tan, 2 **inner basket** pieces (1 in reverse) from medium tan, and 2 **outer basket** pieces (1 in reverse) from dark tan.

ASSEMBLING THE WALL HANGING TOP

*Follow **Piecing and Pressing**, page 113, to make wall hanging top.*

1. Assemble **squares** to make **Unit 1**. Use a compass or plate to mark a 9¹/₂" diameter circle in center of **Unit 1**. Cut out circle to make **Topiary Unit**.

Unit 1

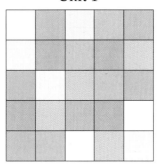

Topiary Unit

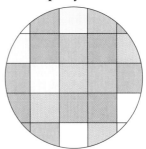

2. Using fabric glue to secure edges of **Topiary Unit**, follow **Invisible Appliqué**, page 116, to stitch all pieces to **background**.
3. Attach **side**, then **top** and **bottom inner borders** to **background**.
4. Attach **top**, **bottom**, then **side outer borders** to complete **Wall Hanging Top**.

COMPLETING THE WALL HANGING

1. Follow **Quilting**, page 119, to mark, layer, and quilt, using **Quilting Diagram** as a suggestion. Our wall hanging is hand quilted using **Border Pattern**, page 84, and **Bow** and **Streamer Patterns**, page 85.

2. Follow **Making a Hanging Sleeve**, page 125, to attach hanging sleeve.

3. Follow **Binding**, page 123, to bind wall hanging using $2^1/2$"w straight-grain binding with overlapped corners.

Wall Hanging Top Diagram

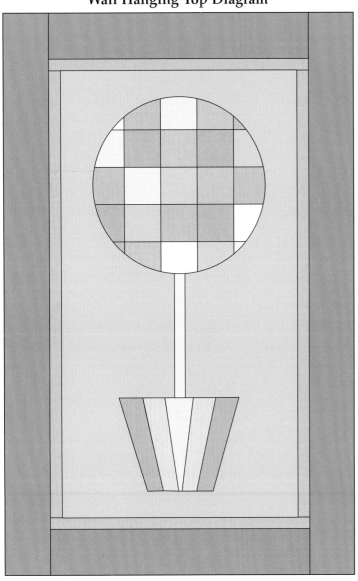

Quilting Diagram

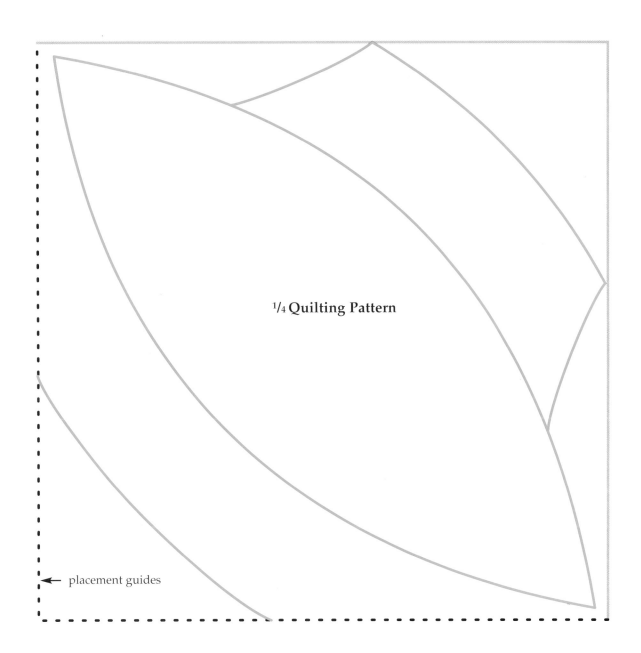

¼ Quilting Pattern

← placement guides

84

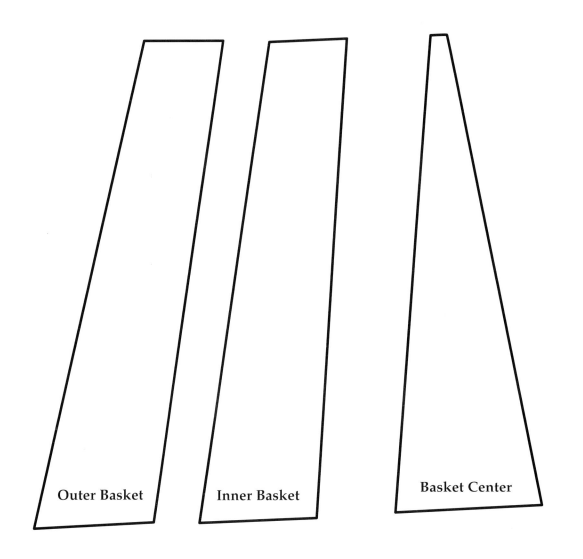

Outer Basket   Inner Basket   Basket Center

Border Pattern

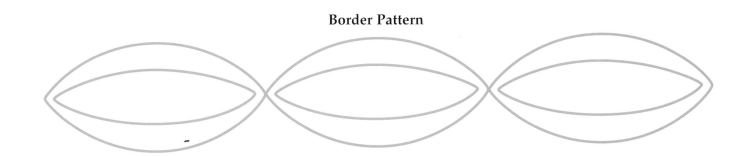

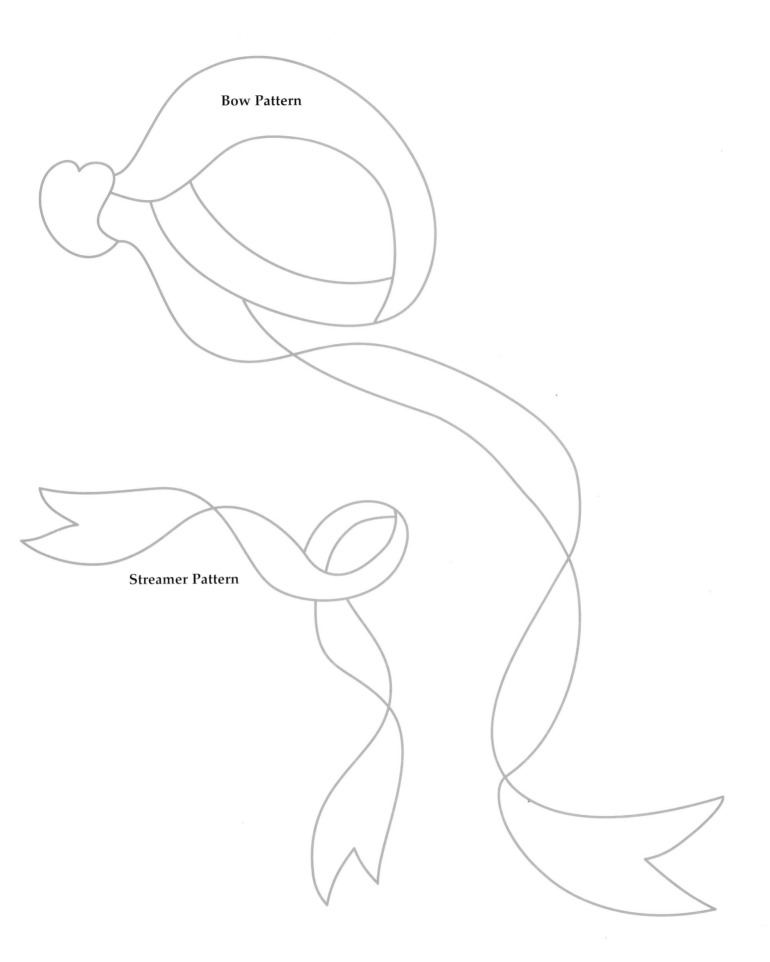

Bow Pattern

Streamer Pattern

Pansies *and* Pinwheels

Bright pinwheels spin while pansies nod in cheerful agreement — with such happy sights surrounding you, pleasant mornings are guaranteed! Color unifies our Pinwheel block quilt with the friendly faces of appliquéd pansies on a wall hanging and throw pillow.

PINWHEEL QUILT

SKILL LEVEL: 1 2 3 4 5
BLOCK SIZE: 8" x 8"
QUILT SIZE: 83" x 99"

YARDAGE REQUIREMENTS

Yardage is based on 45" wide fabric.

- $3^1/2$ yds of purple solid
- $3^3/8$ yds of yellow solid
- $3^1/4$ yds of white solid
- $2^7/8$ yds of blue solid
- $7/8$ yd of light purple solid
  $7^5/8$ yds for backing
  1 yd for binding
  90" x 108" batting

CUTTING OUT THE PIECES

All measurements include a 1/4" seam allowance. Follow Rotary Cutting, page 110, to cut fabric.

1. **From purple solid:**
   - Cut 5 strips $4^7/8$"w. From these strips, cut 40 squares $4^7/8$" x $4^7/8$". Cut squares once diagonally to make 80 **large triangles**.
   - Cut 2 lengthwise **side middle borders** $2^3/4$" x 87".
   - Cut 2 lengthwise **top/bottom middle borders** $2^3/4$" x 76".
   - Cut 4 strips 11"w. From these strips, cut 7 **rectangles** 11" x 16" for triangle-squares.

2. **From yellow solid:**
   - Cut 5 strips $5^1/4$"w. From these strips, cut 40 squares $5^1/4$" x $5^1/4$". Cut squares twice diagonally to make 160 **small triangles**.
   - Cut 2 lengthwise **side inner borders** 2" x 84".
   - Cut 2 lengthwise **top/bottom inner borders** 2" x 71".

3. **From white solid:**
   - Cut 7 strips 11"w. From these strips, cut 14 **rectangles** 11" x 16" for triangle-squares.
   - Cut 5 strips $5^1/4$"w. From these strips, cut 40 squares $5^1/4$" x $5^1/4$". Cut squares twice diagonally to make 160 **small triangles**.

4. **From blue solid:**
   - Cut 2 lengthwise **side outer borders** $5^1/2$" x 92".
   - Cut 2 lengthwise **top/bottom outer borders** $5^1/2$" x 86".
   - Cut 7 **rectangles** 11" x 16" for triangle-squares.

5. **From light purple solid:**
   - Cut 5 strips $4^7/8$"w. From these strips, cut 40 squares $4^7/8$" x $4^7/8$". Cut squares once diagonally to make 80 **large triangles**.

ASSEMBLING THE QUILT TOP

Follow Piecing and Pressing, page 1   to make quilt top.

1. To make triangle-squares, place white and 1 purple **rectangle** right sides together. Referring to **Fig. 1**, follow **Making Triangle-Squares**, page 114 to make 12 **purple triangle-squares**. Repeat with remaining **rectangles** to make a total of 84 **purple triangle-squares** and 84 **blue triangle-squares**. (From each color combination, you will need 80 and have 4 left over.)

Fig. 1

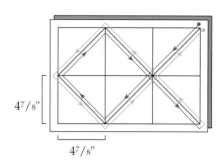

purple triangle-square (make 84)   **blue triangle-square** (make 84)

2. Sew 4 **triangle-squares** together to make **Block A** Make 40 **Block A's**.

Block A (make 40)

3. Sew 2 **small triangles** together to make **Unit 1**. Make 160 **Unit 1's**.

Unit 1 (make 160)

4. Sew 1 **Unit 1** and 1 **large triangle** together to make **Unit 2**. Make 80 **Unit 2's**.

Unit 2 (make 80)

5. Sew 1 **Unit 1** and 1 **large triangle** together to make **Unit 3**. Make 80 **Unit 3's**.

Unit 3 (make 80)

Sew 2 **Unit 2's** and 2 **Unit 3's** together to make **Block B**. Make 40 **Block B's**.

Block B (make 40)

Referring to **Quilt Top Diagram**, sew 4 **Block A's** and 4 **Block B's** together to make **Row**. Make 10 **Rows**.

Row (make 10)

Referring to **Quilt Top Diagram**, sew **Rows** together to make center section of quilt top. Follow **Adding Squared Borders**, page 118, to sew **side**, then **top** and **bottom inner borders** to center section. Repeat to add **middle** and **outer borders** to complete **Quilt Top**.

COMPLETING THE QUILT

1. Follow **Quilting**, page 119, to mark, layer, and quilt using **Quilting Diagram** as a suggestion. Our quilt is hand quilted.
2. Cut a 32" square of binding fabric. Follow **Binding**, page 123, to bind quilt using $2^1/_2$"w bias binding with mitered corners.

Quilting Diagram

Quilt Top Diagram

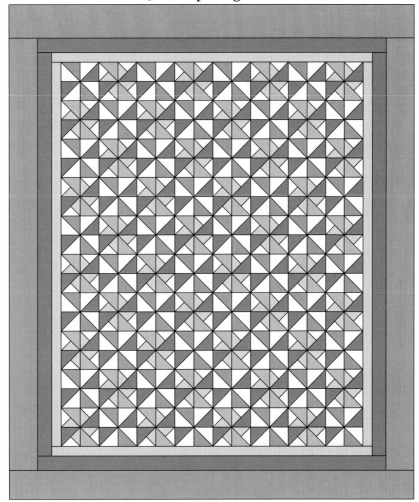

PANSY WALL HANGING

SKILL LEVEL: 1 2 3 4 5
BLOCK SIZE: 11" x 11"
WALL HANGING SIZE: 31" x 44"

YARDAGE REQUIREMENTS

Yardage is based on 45"w fabric.

- $1^1/2$ yds of blue solid
- $3/4$ yd of white solid
- $1/2$ yd of dark green solid
- 1 fat quarter (18" x 22" piece) *each* of light green, very light purple, light purple, purple, dark purple, navy, light yellow, yellow, and dark yellow
- $1^1/2$ yds for backing and hanging sleeve
- $1/2$ yd for binding
- 34" x 48" batting

You will also need:
- template plastic
- $1/4$"w bias pressing bar
- purple embroidery floss

CUTTING OUT THE PIECES

All measurements include a $1/4$" seam allowance. Follow Rotary Cutting, page 110, to cut fabric.

- **From blue solid:**
  - Cut 2 lengthwise **side borders** 3" x 47".
  - Cut 1 **long sashing strip** 3" x $38^1/2$".
  - Cut 2 **top/bottom borders** 3" x 34".
  - Cut 4 **short sashing strips** 3" x $11^1/2$".
- **From white solid:**
  - Cut 2 strips $11^1/2$"w. From these strips, cut 6 **background squares** $11^1/2$" x $11^1/2$".
- **From dark green solid:**
  - Cut 1 **square** 16" x 16" for bias strip.

ASSEMBLING THE WALL HANGING TOP

Follow Piecing and Pressing, page 113, to make wall hanging top.

1. Use patterns, page 95, and follow Step 1 of **Template Cutting**, page 112, to make 1 template *each* of patterns **A - L**.

2. Using **Block** diagram, page 92, as a suggestion for fabric colors, refer to **Hand Appliqué**, page 117, to make appliqués. For *each* **Block**, you will need:

4 **A's**	3 **G's**
4 **B's**	2 **H's**
4 **C's**	2 **I's**
3 **D's** (1 in reverse)	1 **J**
3 **E's** (1 in reverse)	2 **K's** (1 in reverse)
3 **F's** (1 in reverse)	2 **L's** (1 in reverse)

3. To make bias tube for stems, use **square** and follow Steps 1 - 6 of **Making Continuous Bias Strip Binding**, page 123, to make 1"w continuous bias strip.

4. Fold bias strip in half lengthwise with wrong sides together; do not press. Stitch $1/4$" from long raw edge to form tube; trim seam allowance to $1/8$". Place bias pressing bar inside 1 end of tube. Center seam at back of bar and press as you move bar down length of tube. Cut tube to desired lengths for stems.

5. Following **Block** diagram to layer and arrange appliqués and stem pieces on **background square**, refer to **Hand Appliqué**, page 117, to stitch appliqués to background square to complete **Block**. Make 6 **Blocks**.

Block (make 6)

Row (make 2)

6. On *each* **Block,** use 3 strands of embroidery floss and **Satin Stitch**, page 127, to work a $1/4$" circle in the center of each open pansy.
7. Sew 3 **Blocks** and 2 **short sashing strips** together to make vertical **Row**. Make 2 **Rows**.

8. Sew **Rows** and **long sashing strip** together to make center section of wall hanging.
9. Referring to **Wall Hanging Top Diagram**, follow **Adding Mitered Borders**, page 119, to add **borders** to complete **Wall Hanging Top**.

COMPLETING THE WALL HANGING

1. Follow **Quilting**, page 119, to mark, layer, and quilt wall hanging using **Quilting Diagram** as a suggestion. Our wall hanging is hand quilted.
2. Follow **Making a Hanging Sleeve**, page 125, to attach hanging sleeve to wall hanging.
3. Follow **Binding**, page 123, to bind wall hanging using $1^1/_2$"w bias binding with mitered corners.

Quilting Diagram

Wall Hanging Top Diagram

PANSY BOUQUET PILLOW

PILLOW SIZE: 16" x 16"

SUPPLIES

$11^1/2$" x $11^1/2$" **background square** of white solid fabric

4 strips 3" x 17" of blue solid fabric for **borders**

18" x 18" square of fabric for pillow top backing

$16^1/2$" x $16^1/2$" square of fabric for pillow back

scraps of assorted fabrics for appliqués

28" of 1"w bias fabric strip for stems

2 yds of 2"w bias fabric strip for welting

2 yds of $^1/4$" cord for welting

template plastic

$^1/4$"w bias pressing bar

purple embroidery floss

polyester fiberfill

MAKING THE PILLOW

*Refer to photo and follow **Piecing and Pressing**, page 113, to make pillow.*

1. Follow Steps 1 and 2 of **Assembling the Wall Hanging Top**, page 91, to make appliqués for 1 **Block**.
2. Use 1"w bias strip and refer to Steps 4 and 5 of **Assembling the Wall Hanging Top**, page 91, to make bias tube for stems and to complete 1 **Block**.
3. Follow **Adding Mitered Borders**, page 119, to sew **borders** to **Block** to complete **Pillow Top**.

4. Use 3 strands of embroidery floss and **Satin Stitch**, page 127, to work a $^1/4$" circle in the center of each open pansy.
5. Follow **Quilting**, page 119, to mark, layer, and quilt pillow top. Our pillow top is hand quilted in the ditch around appliqués and at $^1/2$" intervals outside appliquéd motif.
6. Follow **Pillow Finishing**, page 126, to complete pillow with welting.

Pillow Top Diagram

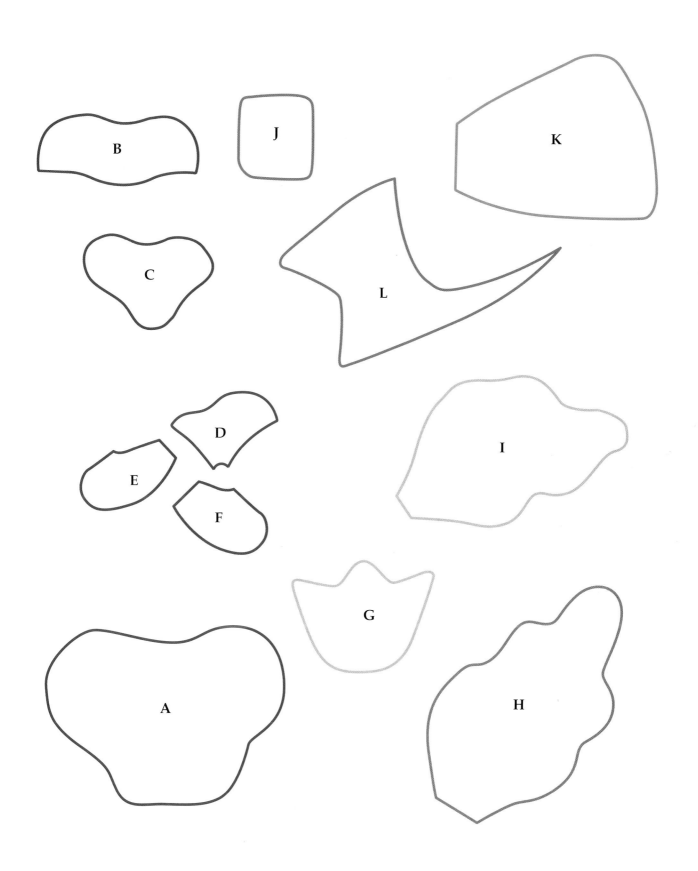

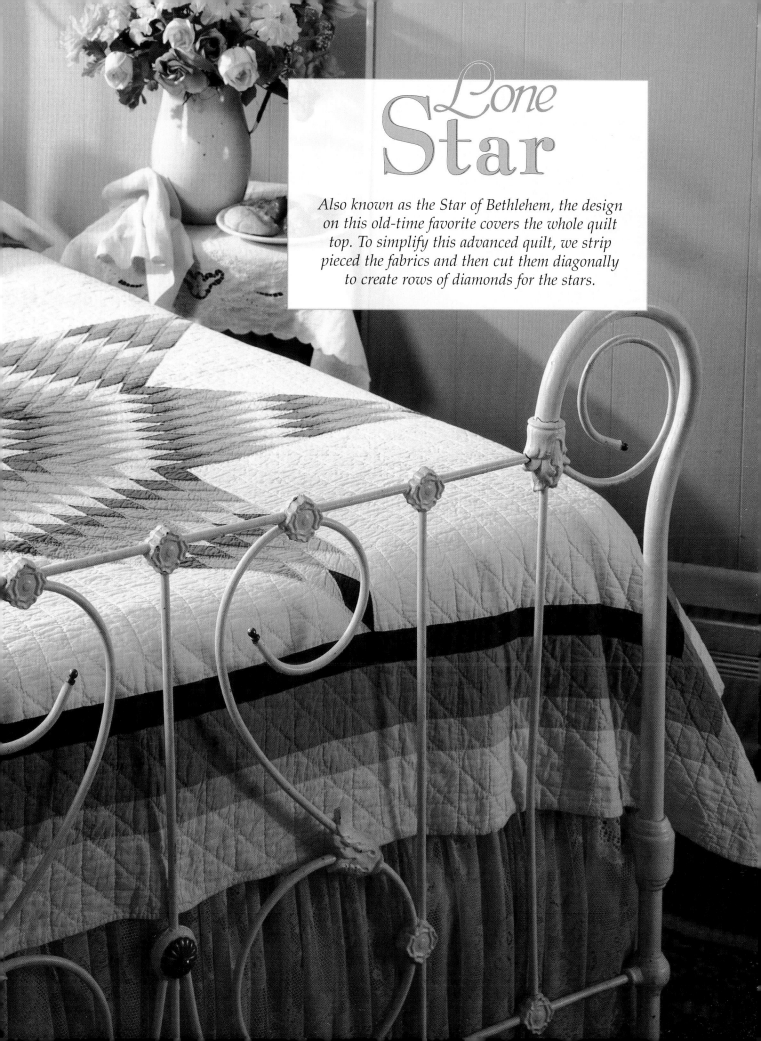

Lone Star

Also known as the Star of Bethlehem, the design on this old-time favorite covers the whole quilt top. To simplify this advanced quilt, we strip pieced the fabrics and then cut them diagonally to create rows of diamonds for the stars.

LONE STAR QUILT

SKILL LEVEL: 1 2 3 4 5
QUILT SIZE: 82" x 82"

YARDAGE REQUIREMENTS

Yardage is based on 45"w fabric.

- ☐ 3¹/₂ yds of white
- ☐ 2³/₄ yds of light pink
- ☐ 2³/₄ yds of pink
- ☐ 2³/₄ yds of purple
- ☐ 2³/₄ yds of blue
  7 yds for backing
  1 yd for binding
  90" x 108" batting

CUTTING OUT THE PIECES

All measurements include a ¹/₄" seam allowance. Follow Rotary Cutting, page 110, to cut fabric.

1. **From white:** ☐
   - Cut 4 lengthwise strips 4" x 89" for **borders**.
   - Cut 4 squares 19³/₄" x 19³/₄" for **corner squares**.

corner square (cut 4)

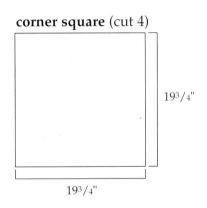

19³/₄"

19³/₄"

   - Cut 1 square 28¹/₄" x 28¹/₄". Cut square twice diagonally to make 4 **side triangles**.

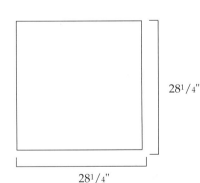

28¹/₄"

28¹/₄"

side triangles (cut 4)

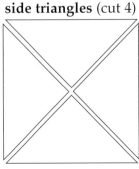

28¹/₄"

2. **From light pink:** ☐
   - Cut 4 lengthwise strips 2" x 89" for **borders**.
   - Cut 20 **strips** 2"w x remaining fabric width.

3. **From pink:** ☐
   - Cut 4 lengthwise strips 2" x 89" for **borders**.
   - Cut 20 **strips** 2"w x remaining fabric width.

4. **From purple:** ☐
   - Cut 4 lengthwise strips 2" x 89" for **borders**.
   - Cut 20 **strips** 2"w x remaining fabric width.

5. **From blue:** ☐
   - Cut 4 lengthwise strips 2" x 89" for **borders**.
   - Cut 21 **strips** 2"w x remaining fabric width.

ASSEMBLING THE QUILT TOP

Follow Piecing and Pressing, page 113, to make quilt top.

1. Assemble each strip set in the color order shown, adding each new **strip** 1¹/₂" from the end of the previous strip to make **Strip Sets A, B, C, and D**. Make 3 **Strip Set A's** and 2 each of **Strip Sets B,** and **D**.

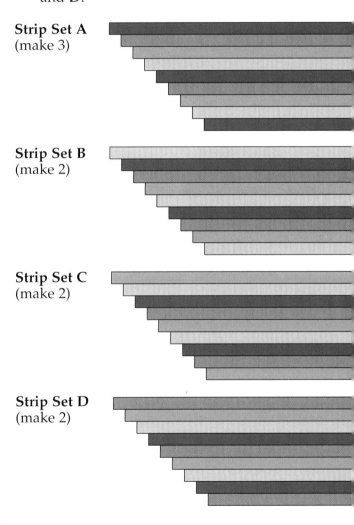

Strip Set A
(make 3)

Strip Set B
(make 2)

Strip Set C
(make 2)

Strip Set D
(make 2)

Referring to **Fig. 1**, use a large right-angle triangle aligned with a seam to determine an accurate 45° cutting line. Use rotary cutter and rotary cutting ruler to trim the uneven ends from one end of each **Strip Set**.

Fig. 1

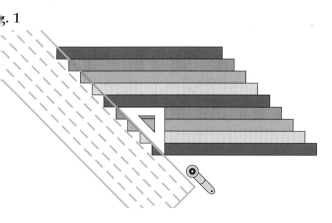

Aligning the 45° mark on the rotary cutting ruler (shown in pink) with a seam and aligning the 2" mark with the edge of the cut made in Step 2, cut across **Strip Sets** at 2" intervals as shown in **Fig. 2**.

Fig. 2

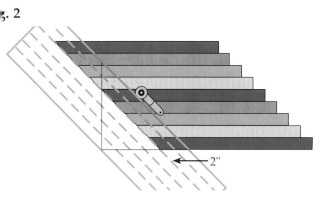

From **Strip Set A's**, cut a total of 24 **Unit 1's**.

Unit 1 (cut 24)

From **Strip Set B's**, cut a total of 16 **Unit 2's**.

Unit 2 (cut 16)

From **Strip Set C's**, cut a total of 16 **Unit 3's**.

Unit 3 (cut 16)

From **Strip Set D's**, cut a total of 16 **Unit 4's**.

Unit 4 (cut 16)

4. When making **Unit 5's**, refer to **Fig. 3** to match long edges of units. Seams will cross $1/4$" from cut edges of fabric. Pin and stitch as shown in **Fig. 3**. Assemble 3 **Unit 1's**, 2 **Unit 2's**, 2 **Unit 3's**, and 2 **Unit 4's** in order shown to make **Unit 5**. Make 8 **Unit 5's**.

Fig. 3

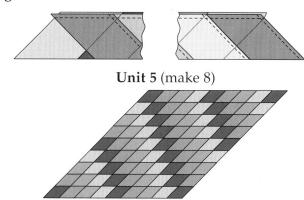

Unit 5 (make 8)

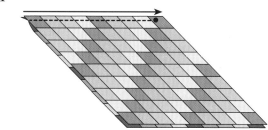

5. To make **Unit 6**, place 2 **Unit 5's** right sides together, carefully matching edges and seams; pin. Stitch in direction shown in **Fig. 4**, ending stitching $1/4$" from edge of fabric (you may find it helpful to mark a small dot at this point before sewing) and backstitching at end of seam. Make 4 **Unit 6's**.

Fig. 4

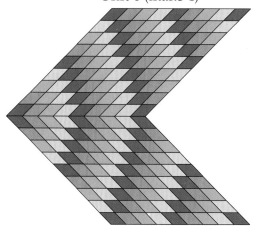

Unit 6 (make 4)

6. Referring to **Quilt Top Diagram**, page 101, assemble **Unit 6's** to make **Star**, always ending stitching $1/4$" from edges and backstitching.
7. Follow **Working With Set-in Seams**, page 115, to attach **corner squares**, then **side triangles**, to **Star** to complete center section of quilt top as shown in **Quilt Top Diagram**.
8. Assemble **borders** as shown to make **Border Unit**. Make 4 **Border Units**.

Border Unit (make 4)

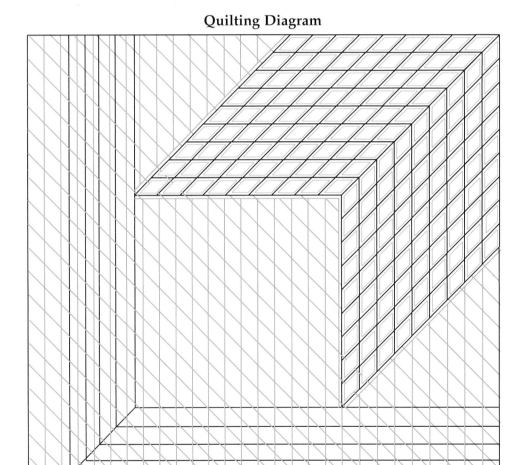

9. Follow **Adding Mitered Borders**, page 119, and attach **Border Units** to complete **Quilt Top**.

COMPLETING THE QUILT

1. Follow **Quilting**, page 119, and **Quilting Diagram** to mark, layer, and quilt. Our quilt is hand quilted.
2. Cut a 36" square of fabric for binding. Follow **Making Continuous Bias Strip Binding**, page 123, to make approximately 10 yds of $2^{1}/2$"w bias binding.
3. Follow **Attaching Binding with Mitered Corners**, page 124, to attach binding to quilt.

Quilting Diagram

Star *of the* Orient

Providing an exciting challenge for the experienced quilter, this intricate pattern features Pineapple borders and eight-pointed, interlocking stars. Small prints give this modern quilt an old-fashioned look.

TAR OF THE ORIENT QUILT

KILL LEVEL: 1 2 3 4 5
LOCK SIZE: 14" x 14"
UILT SIZE: 84" x 98"

ARDAGE REQUIREMENTS

rdage is based on 45"w fabric.

- 4 yds of white
- 1 yd of assorted light pink prints
- 1¹/₂ yd of assorted dark pink prints
- 1⁵/₈ yds of assorted light orange prints
- ⁷/₈ yd of assorted dark orange prints
- 1⁵/₈ yds of assorted light yellow prints
- ⁷/₈ yd of assorted dark yellow prints
- 1³/₈ yds of assorted light green prints
- 1¹/₂ yd of assorted dark green prints
- ³/₄ yd of assorted light blue prints
- 1¹/₄ yd of assorted dark blue prints
- ³/₄ yd of assorted light purple prints
- ³/₄ yd of assorted dark purple prints
- ³/₄ yd of assorted grey prints

6 yds for backing
1¹/₈ yds for binding
90" x 108" batting

UTTING OUT THE PIECES

'l measurements include a ¹/₄" seam allowance. Follow
mplate Cutting, page 112, to make templates from all
tterns on pages 106 and 107. For each of 42 blocks, you
'll need to cut B and C pieces from the same fabric for each
of colors. You will also need 4 matching pieces for pieces
-I. Use templates to cut out the following pieces:

Template A:
- Cut 42 from white fabric.

Template B:
- Cut 42 from each of the assorted colors of dark pinks, light oranges, light yellows, greys, light greens, dark greens, light blues, and light purples.

Template C:
- Cut 42 from each of the assorted colors of dark pinks, light oranges, light yellows, greys, light greens, dark greens, light blues, and light purples (1 to match each **B**).
- Cut 336 from white fabric.

Template D:
- Cut 84 from dark purple prints (cut in sets of 4).
- Cut 84 from dark blue prints (cut in sets of 4).

5. **Template E:**
- Cut 84 from light pink prints (cut in sets of 4).
- Cut 84 from light green prints (cut in sets of 4).

6. **Template F:**
- Cut 84 from dark pink prints (cut in sets of 4).
- Cut 84 from dark green prints (cut in sets of 4).

7. **Template G:**
- Cut 84 from light orange prints (cut in sets of 4).
- Cut 84 from light yellow prints (cut in sets of 4).

8. **Template H:**
- Cut 84 from dark orange prints (cut in sets of 4).
- Cut 84 from dark yellow prints (cut in sets of 4).

9. **Template I:**
- Cut 84 from white.
- Cut 84 from dark blue prints (cut in sets of 4).

ASSEMBLING THE QUILT TOP

Follow Piecing and Pressing, page 113, to make quilt top.

1. Referring to **Fig. 1**, sew dark pink **B** to **A halfway** down 1 side of the octagon.

Fig. 1

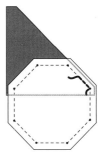

2. Sew 1 light purple **B** to dark pink **B** and **A** as shown in **Fig. 2**. Referring to **Unit 1** diagram for color placement, continue adding **B**'s in a counterclockwise direction, completing first seam when adding last **B** to make **Unit 1**.

Fig. 2   **Unit 1**

3. Using **C** fabrics to match **B** fabrics, sew 1 white **C** to 1 colored **C** to make **Unit 2**. Repeat to make a total of 8 **Unit 2's**.

Unit 2 (make 8)

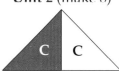

103

4. Referring to **Fig. 3** for color placement, sew dark pink **Unit 2** to **Unit 1** halfway down 1 side of the octagon.

Fig. 3

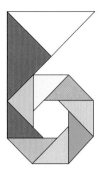

5. Referring to **Unit 3** diagram for color placement, continue adding **Unit 2's** in a counterclockwise direction, completing first seam when adding last **Unit 2** to make **Unit 3**.

Unit 3

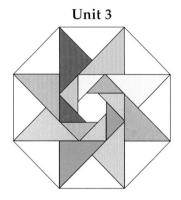

6. Repeat Steps 1-5 to make 42 **Unit 3's**.
7. Referring to **Block #1** and **Block #2** diagrams for color placement, sew pieces **D-I** to **Unit 3's** in alphabetical order. Repeat to make 21 **Block #1's** and 21 **Block #2's**.

Block #1

Block #2

104

Sew 3 **Block #1's** and 3 **Block #2's** together to make **Row 1**. Repeat to make **Rows 2-7**.

Row 1

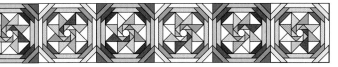

Referring to **Quilt Top Diagram** for placement, sew **Rows 1-7** together to complete **Quilt Top**.

COMPLETING THE QUILT

1. Follow **Choosing and Preparing the Backing** and **Choosing and Preparing the Batting**, page 121, to piece backing if necessary.
2. Follow **Assembling the Quilt**, page 121, to layer backing, batting, and quilt top and to baste all layers together.
3. Follow **Quilting**, page 119, and stitch quilt in the ditch along all seamlines. Our quilt is hand quilted. Trim batting and backing even with edges of quilt.
4. Cut a 36" square of binding fabric. Follow **Binding**, page 123, to bind quilt using 2"w bias binding with mitered corners.

Quilt Top Diagram

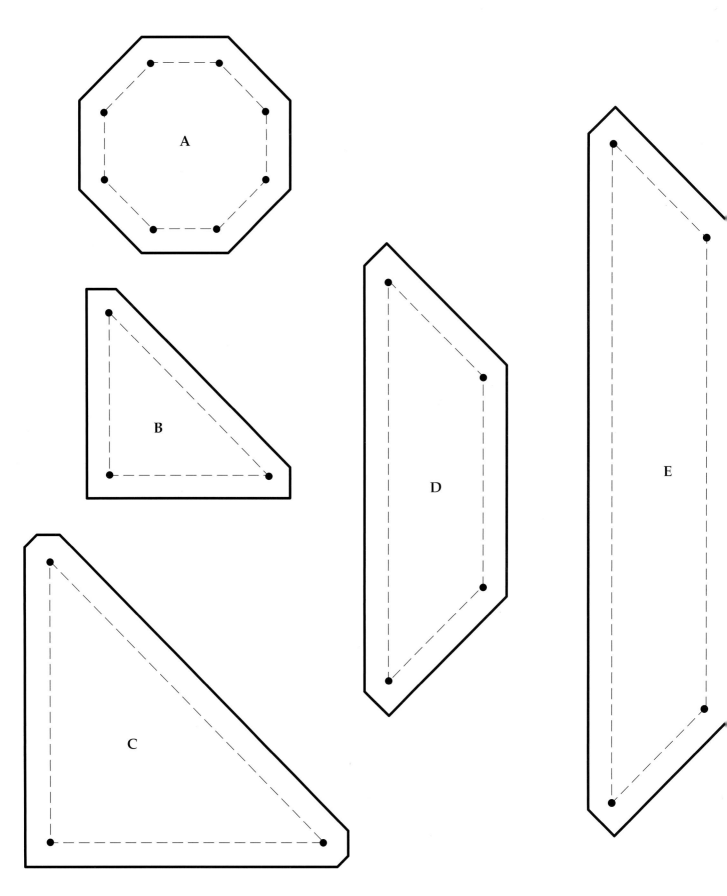

Pattern for Star of the Orient reprinted from
Scrap Quilts by Judy Martin, with permission
from Leman Publications, Inc.

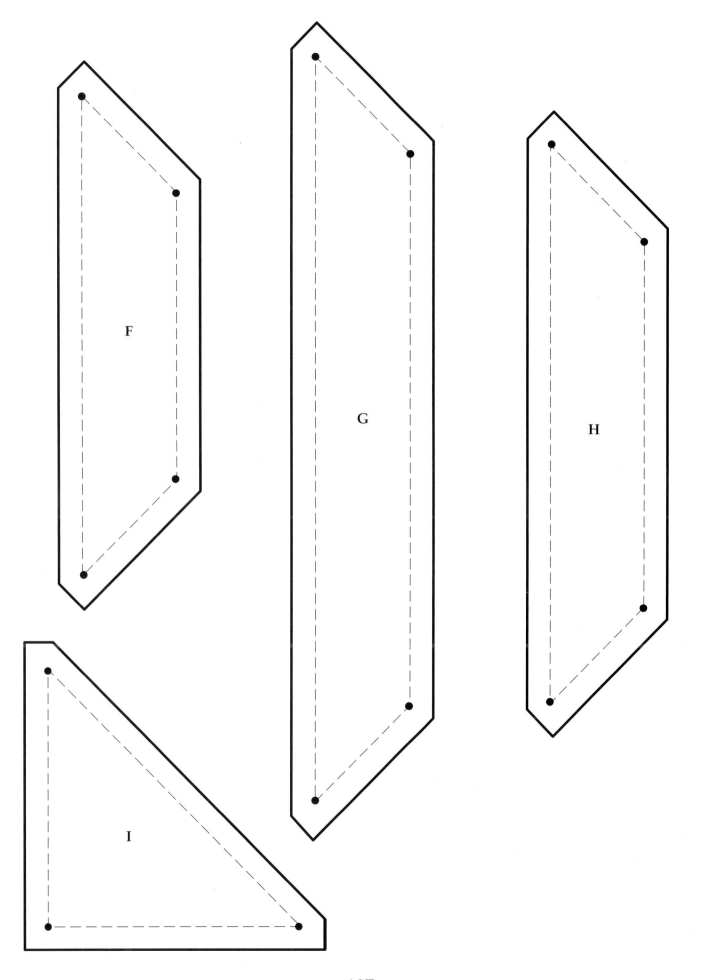

F

G

H

I

107

GENERAL INSTRUCTIONS

Complete instructions are given for making each of the quilts and other projects shown in this book. Skill levels indicated for quilts and wall hangings may help you choose the right project. To make your quilting easier and more enjoyable, we encourage you to carefully read all of the general instructions, study the color photographs, and familiarize yourself with the individual project instructions before beginning a project.

QUILTING SUPPLIES

This list includes all the tools you need for basic quick-method quiltmaking, plus additional supplies used for special techniques. Unless otherwise specified, all items may be found in your favorite fabric store or quilt shop.

Batting — Batting is most commonly available in polyester, cotton, or a polyester/cotton blend (see **Choosing and Preparing the Batting**, page 121).

Cutting mat — A cutting mat is a special mat designed to be used with a rotary cutter. A mat that measures approximately 18" x 24" is a good size for most cutting.

Eraser — A soft white fabric eraser or white art eraser may be used to remove pencil marks from fabric. Do not use a colored eraser, as the dye may discolor fabric.

Iron — An iron with both steam and dry settings and a smooth, clean soleplate is necessary for proper pressing.

Marking tools — There are many different marking tools available (see **Marking Quilting Lines**, page 120). A silver quilter's pencil is a good marker for both light and dark fabrics.

Masking tape — Two widths of masking tape, 1"w and $^1/_4$"w, are helpful when quilting. The 1"w tape is used to secure the backing fabric to a flat surface when layering the quilt. The $^1/_4$"w tape may be used as a guide when outline quilting.

Needles — Two types of needles are used for hand sewing: *Betweens*, used for quilting, are short and strong for stitching through layered fabric and batting. *Sharps* are longer, thinner needles used for basting and other hand sewing. For *sewing machine needles*, we recommend size 10 to 14 or 70 to 90 universal (sharp-pointed) needles.

Paper-backed fusible web — This iron-on adhesive with paper backing is used to secure fabric cutouts to another fabric when appliquéing. If the cutouts will be stitched in place, purchase a lighter weight web that will not gum up your sewing machine needle. A heavier weight web is used for appliqués that are fused in place with no stitching.

Permanent fine-point pen — A permanent pen is used to mark templates and stencils and to sign and date quilts. Test pen on fabric to make sure i will not bleed or wash out.

Pins — Straight pins made especially for quilting are extra long with large round heads. Glass head pins will stand up to occasional contact with a hc iron. Some quilters prefer extra-fine dressmaker' silk pins. If you are machine quilting, you will need a large supply of 1" long (size 01) rustproof safety pins for pin-basting.

Quilting hoop or frame — Quilting hoops and frame are designed to hold the 3 layers of a quilt together securely while you quilt. Many different types and sizes are available, including round an oval wooden hoops, frames made of rigid plastic pipe, and large floor frames made of either material. A 14" or 16" hoop allows you to quilt in your lap and makes your quilting portable.

Rotary cutter — The rotary cutter is the essential too for quick-method quilting techniques. The cutter consists of a round, sharp blade mounted on a handle with a retractable blade guard for safety. I should be used only with a cutting mat and rotar cutting ruler. Two sizes are generally available; w recommend the larger (45 mm) size.

Rotary cutting ruler — A rotary cutting ruler is a thick, clear acrylic ruler made specifically for use with a rotary cutter. It should have accurate $^1/_8$" crosswise and lengthwise markings and marking for 45° and 60° angles. A 6" x 24" ruler is a good size for most cutting. An additional 6" x 12" ruler or 12$^1/_2$" square ruler is helpful when cutting wider pieces. Many specialty rulers are available that make specific cutting tasks faster and easier.

Scissors — Although most fabric cutting will be done with a rotary cutter, sharp, high-quality scissors are still needed for some cutting. A separate pair of scissors for cutting paper and plastic is recommended. Smaller scissors are handy for clipping threads.

seam ripper — A good seam ripper with a fine point is useful for removing stitching.

sewing machine — A sewing machine that produces a good, even straight stitch is all that is necessary for most quilting. Zigzag stitch capability is necessary for **Invisible Appliqué**, page 116. Clean and oil your machine often and keep the tension set properly.

stabilizer — Commercially made, non-woven material or paper stabilizer is placed behind background fabric when doing **Invisible Appliqué**, page 116, to provide a more stable stitching surface.

tape measure — A flexible 120" long tape measure is helpful for measuring a quilt top before adding borders.

template material — Sheets of translucent plastic, often pre-marked with a grid, are made especially for making templates and quilting stencils.

thimble — A thimble is necessary when hand quilting. Thimbles are available in metal, plastic, or leather and in many sizes and styles. Choose a thimble that fits well and is comfortable.

thread — Several types of thread are used for quiltmaking: *General-purpose* sewing thread is used for basting, piecing, and some appliquéing. Choose high-quality cotton or cotton-covered polyester thread in light and dark neutrals, such as ecru and grey, for your basic supplies. *Quilting* thread is stronger than general-purpose sewing thread, and some brands have a coating to make them slide more easily through the quilt layers. Some machine appliqué projects in this book use *transparent monofilament* (clear nylon) thread. Use a very fine (.004 mm) soft nylon thread that is not stiff or wiry. Choose clear nylon thread for white or light fabrics or smoke nylon thread for darker fabrics.

triangle — A large plastic right-angle triangle (available in art and office supply stores) is useful in rotary cutting for making first cuts to "square up" raw edges of fabric and for checking to see that cuts remain at right angles to the fold.

walking foot — A walking foot, or even-feed foot, is needed for straight-line machine quilting. This special foot will help all 3 layers move at the same rate over the feed dogs to provide a smoother quilted project.

FABRICS

SELECTING FABRICS

Choose high-quality, medium-weight 100% cotton fabrics such as broadcloth or calico. All-cotton fabrics hold a crease better, fray less, and are easier to quilt than cotton/polyester blends. All the fabrics for a quilt should be of comparable weight and weave. Check the end of the fabric bolt for fiber content and width.

The yardage requirements listed for each project are based on 45" wide fabric with a "usable" width of 42" after shrinkage and trimming selvages. Your actual usable width will probably vary slightly from fabric to fabric. Though most fabrics will yield 42" or more, if you find a fabric that you suspect will yield a narrower usable width, you will need to purchase additional yardage to compensate. Our recommended yardage lengths should be adequate for occasional resquaring of fabric when many cuts are required, but it never hurts to buy a little more fabric for insurance against a narrower usable width, the occasional cutting error, or to have on hand for making coordinating projects.

PREPARING FABRICS

All fabrics should be washed, dried, and pressed before cutting.

1. To check colorfastness before washing, cut a small piece of the fabric and place in a glass of hot water with a little detergent. Leave fabric in the water for a few minutes. Remove fabric from water and blot with white paper towels. If any color bleeds onto the towels, wash the fabric separately with warm water and detergent, then rinse until the water runs clear. If fabric continues to bleed, choose another fabric.

2. Unfold yardage and separate fabrics by color. To help reduce raveling, use scissors to snip a small triangle from each corner of your fabric pieces. Machine wash fabrics in warm water with a small amount of mild laundry detergent. Do not use fabric softener. Rinse well and then dry fabrics in the dryer, checking long fabric lengths occasionally to make sure they are not tangling.

3. To make ironing easier, remove fabrics from dryer while they are slightly damp. Refold each fabric lengthwise (as it was on the bolt) with wrong sides together and matching selvages. If necessary, adjust slightly at selvages so that fold lays flat. Press each fabric using a steam iron set on "Cotton."

ROTARY CUTTING

*Based on the idea that you can easily cut strips of fabric and then cut those strips into smaller pieces, rotary cutting has brought speed and accuracy to quiltmaking. Observe safety precautions when using the rotary cutter, since it is extremely sharp. Develop a habit of retracting the blade guard **just before** making a cut and closing it **immediately afterward**, before laying down the cutter.*

1. Follow **Preparing Fabrics**, page 109, to wash, dry, and press fabrics.
2. Cut all strips from the selvage-to-selvage width of the fabric unless otherwise indicated in project instructions. Place fabric on the cutting mat, as shown in **Fig. 1**, with the fold of the fabric toward you. To straighten the uneven fabric edge, make the first "squaring up" cut by placing the right edge of the rotary cutting ruler over the left raw edge of the fabric. Place right-angle triangle (or another rotary cutting ruler) with the lower edge carefully aligned with the fold and the left edge against the ruler (**Fig. 1**). Hold the ruler firmly with your left hand, placing your little finger off the left edge to anchor the ruler. Remove the triangle, pick up the rotary cutter, and retract the blade guard. Using a smooth downward motion, make the cut by running the blade of the rotary cutter firmly along the right edge of the ruler (**Fig. 2**). **Always** cut in a direction **away** from your body and **immediately** close the blade guard after each cut.

Fig. 2

3. To cut each of the strips required for a project, place the ruler over the cut edge of the fabric, aligning desired marking on the ruler with the cut edge (**Fig. 3**); make the cut. When cutting several strips from a single piece of fabric, it is important to occasionally use the ruler and triangle to ensure that cuts are still at a perfect right angle to the fold. If not, repeat Step 2 to straighten.

Fig. 3

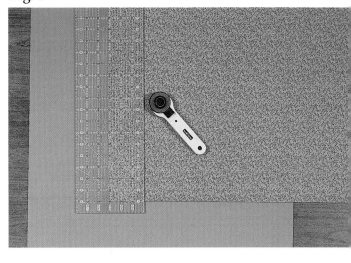

Fig. 1

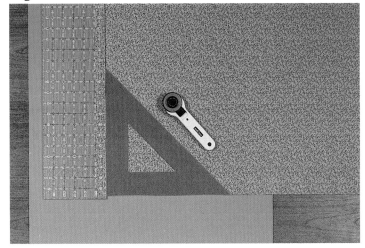

4. To square up selvage ends of a strip before cutting pieces, refer to **Fig. 4** and place folded strip on mat with selvage ends to your right. Aligning a horizontal marking on ruler with 1 long edge of strip, use rotary cutter to trim selvage to make end of strip square and even (**Fig. 4**). Turn strip (or entire mat) so that cut end is to your left before making subsequent cuts.

Fig. 4

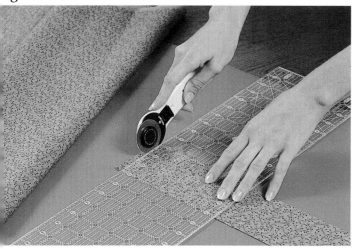

Pieces such as rectangles and squares can now be cut from strips. (Cutting other shapes such as diamonds is discussed in individual project instructions.) Usually strips remain folded, and pieces are cut in pairs after ends of strips are squared up. To cut squares or rectangles from a strip, place ruler over left end of strip, aligning desired marking on ruler with cut end of strip. To ensure perfectly square cuts, align a horizontal marking on ruler with 1 long edge of strip (**Fig. 5**) before making the cut.

Fig. 5

6. To cut 2 triangles from a square, cut square the size indicated in the project instructions. Cut square once diagonally to make 2 triangles (**Fig. 6**).

Fig. 6

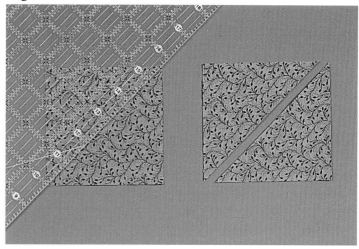

7. To cut 4 triangles from a square, cut square the size indicated in the project instructions. Cut square twice diagonally to make 4 triangles (**Fig. 7**). You may find it helpful to use a small rotary cutting mat so that the mat can be turned to make second cut without disturbing fabric pieces.

Fig. 7

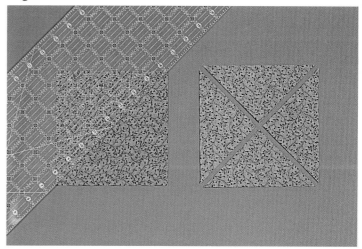

8. After some practice, you may want to try stacking up to 6 fabric layers when making cuts. When stacking strips, match long cut edges and follow Step 4 to square up ends of strip stack. Carefully turn stack (or entire mat) so that squared-up ends are to your left before making subsequent cuts. After cutting, check accuracy of pieces. Some shapes, such as diamonds, are more difficult to cut accurately in stacks.

9. In some cases, strips will be sewn together into strip sets before being cut into smaller units. When cutting a strip set, align a seam in strip set with a horizontal marking on the ruler to maintain square cuts (**Fig. 8**). We do not recommend stacking strip sets for rotary cutting.

Fig. 8

10. Most borders for quilts in this book are cut along the more stable lengthwise grain to minimize wavy edges caused by stretching. To remove selvages before cutting lengthwise strips, place fabric on mat with selvages to your left and squared-up end at bottom of mat. Placing ruler over selvage and using squared-up edge instead of fold, follow Step 2 to cut away selvages as you did raw edges (**Fig. 9**). After making a cut the length of the mat, move the next section of fabric to be cut onto the mat. Repeat until you have removed selvages from required length of fabric.

Fig. 9

11. After removing selvages, place ruler over left edge of fabric, aligning desired marking on ruler with cut edge of fabric. Make cuts as in Step 3. After each cut move next section of fabric onto mat as in Step 10.

TEMPLATE CUTTING

Our full-sized piecing template patterns have 2 lines – a solid cutting line and a dashed line showing the 1/4" seam allowance. Patterns for appliqué templates do not include seam allowances.

1. To make a template from a pattern, use a permanent fine-point pen to carefully trace pattern onto template plastic, making sure to transfer all alignment and grain line markings. Cut out template along inner edge of drawn line. Check template against original pattern for accuracy.

2. To make a template from a one-quarter pattern, use a ruler to draw a line down the center of a sheet of template plastic. Turn plastic 90° and draw a line down the center, perpendicular to the first line. Match grey lines of pattern to intersection of lines of plastic. Trace pattern. Turn plastic and trace pattern in remaining corners. Cut out template as in Step 1.

3. To use a template, place template on wrong side of fabric (unless otherwise indicated in project instructions), aligning grain line on template with straight grain of fabric. Use a sharp fabric-marking pencil to draw around template. Transfer all alignment markings to fabric. Cut out fabric piece using scissors or rotary cutting equipment.

PIECING AND PRESSING

Precise cutting, followed by accurate piecing and careful pressing, will ensure that all the pieces of your quilt top fit together well.

PIECING

Set sewing machine stitch length for approximately 11 stitches per inch. Use a new, sharp needle suited for medium-weight woven fabric.

Use a neutral-colored general-purpose sewing thread (not quilting thread) in the needle and in the bobbin. Stitch first on a scrap of fabric to check upper and bobbin thread tension; make any adjustments necessary.

For good results, it is **essential** that you stitch with an **accurate ¼" seam allowance**. On many sewing machines, the measurement from the needle to the outer edge of the presser foot is ¼". If this is the case with your machine, the presser foot is your best guide. If not, measure ¼" from the needle and mark throat plate with a piece of masking tape. Special presser feet that are exactly ¼" wide are also available for most sewing machines.

When piecing, **always** place pieces **right sides together** and **match raw edges**; pin if necessary. (If using straight pins, remove the pins just before they reach the sewing machine needle.)

Chain Piecing

Chain piecing whenever possible will make your work go faster and will usually result in more accurate piecing. Stack the pieces you will be sewing beside your machine in the order you will need them and in a position that will allow you to easily pick them up. Pick up each pair of pieces, carefully place them together as they will be sewn, and feed them into the machine one after the other. Stop between each pair only long enough to pick up the next pair; don't cut thread between pairs (**Fig. 10**). After all pieces are sewn, cut threads, press, and go on to the next step, chain piecing when possible.

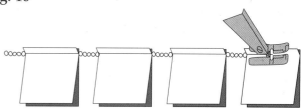

Fig. 10

Sewing Strip Sets

When there are several strips to assemble into a strip set, first sew the strips together into pairs, then sew the pairs together to form the strip set. To help avoid distortion, sew 1 seam in 1 direction and then sew the next seam in the opposite direction (**Fig. 11**).

Fig. 11

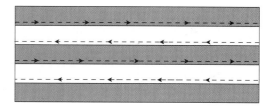

Sewing Across Seam Intersections

When sewing across the intersection of 2 seams, place pieces right sides together and match seams exactly, making sure seam allowances are pressed in opposite directions (**Fig. 12**). To prevent fabric from shifting, you may wish to pin in place.

Fig. 12

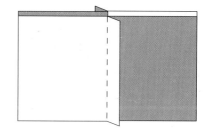

Sewing Bias Seams

Care should be used in handling and stitching bias edges since they stretch easily. After sewing the seam, carefully press seam allowance to 1 side, making sure not to stretch fabric.

Sewing Sharp Points

To ensure sharp points when joining triangular or diagonal pieces, stitch across the center of the "X" (shown in pink) formed on the wrong side by previous seams (**Fig. 13**).

Fig. 13

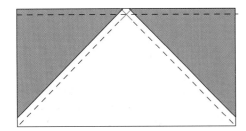

Making Triangle-Squares

The grid method for making triangle-squares is faster and more accurate than cutting and sewing individual triangles. Stitching before cutting the triangle-squares apart also prevents stretching the bias edges.

1. Follow project instructions to cut rectangles or squares of fabric for making triangle-squares. Place the indicated pieces right sides together and press.
2. On the wrong side of the lighter fabric, draw a grid of squares similar to that shown in **Fig. 14**. The size and number of squares are given in the project instructions.

Fig. 14

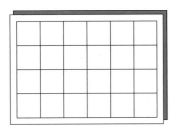

3. Following the example given in the project instructions, draw 1 diagonal line through each square in the grid (**Fig. 15**).

Fig. 15

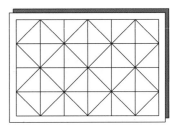

4. Stitch $1/4$" on each side of all diagonal lines. For accuracy, it may be helpful to first draw your stitching lines onto the fabric, especially if your presser foot is not your $1/4$" guide. In some cases, stitching may be done in a single continuous line. Project instructions include a diagram similar to **Fig. 16**, which shows stitching lines and the direction of the stitching.

Fig. 16

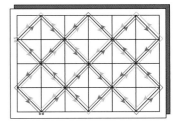

5. Use rotary cutter and ruler to cut along all drawn lines of the grid. Each square of the grid will yield 2 triangle-squares (**Fig. 17**).

Fig. 17

6. Carefully press triangle-squares open, pressing seam allowances toward darker fabric. Trim points of seam allowances that extend beyond edges of triangle-square (see **Fig. 22**).

orking with Set-in Seams

cing diamonds and parallelograms requires special dling. For best results, carefully follow the steps below.

When sewing 2 diamond or parallelogram pieces together, place pieces right sides together, carefully matching edges; pin. Mark a small dot $^1/_4$" from corner of 1 piece as shown in **Fig. 18**. Stitch pieces together in the direction shown, stopping at center of dot and backstitching.

. 18

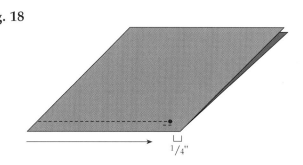

For best results, add side triangles, then corner squares to diamond or parallelogram sections. Mark corner of each piece to be set in with a small dot (**Fig. 19**).

. 19

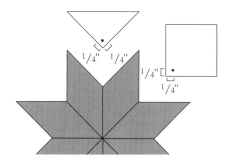

To sew first seam, match right sides and pin the triangle or square to the diamond or parallelogram on the left. Stitch seam from outer edge to the dot, backstitching at dot; clip threads (**Fig. 20**).

. 20

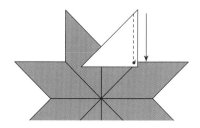

4. To sew the second seam, pivot the added triangle or square to match raw edges of next diamond or parallelogram. Beginning at dot, take 2 or 3 stitches, then backstitch, making sure not to backstitch into previous seam allowance. Continue stitching to outer edge (**Fig. 21**).

Fig. 21

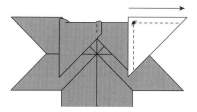

Trimming Seam Allowances

When sewing with diamond or triangle pieces, some seam allowances may extend beyond the edges of the sewn pieces. Trim away "dog ears" that extend beyond the edges of the sewn pieces (**Fig. 22**).

Fig. 22

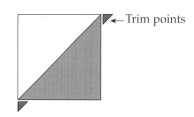

← Trim points

PRESSING

Use a steam iron set on "Cotton" for all pressing. Press as you sew, taking care to prevent small folds along seamlines. Seam allowances are almost always pressed to one side, usually toward the darker fabric. However, to reduce bulk it may occasionally be necessary to press seam allowances toward the lighter fabric or even to press them open. In order to prevent a dark fabric seam allowance from showing through a light fabric, trim the darker seam allowance slightly narrower than the lighter seam allowance. To press long seams, such as those in long strip sets, without curving or other distortion, lay strips across the width of the ironing board.

APPLIQUÉ

PREPARING APPLIQUÉ PIECES

Patterns are printed in reverse to enable you to use our speedy method of preparing appliqués. This method can be used when securing appliqués with Invisible Appliqué. White or light-colored fabrics may need to be lined with fusible interfacing before applying fusible web to prevent darker fabrics from showing through.

1. Place paper-backed fusible web, web side down, over appliqué pattern. Use a pencil to trace pattern onto paper side of web as many times as indicated in project instructions for a single fabric. Repeat for additional patterns and fabrics.
2. Follow manufacturer's instructions to fuse traced patterns to wrong side of fabrics. Do not remove paper backing. (*Note:* Some pieces may be given as measurements, such as a 2" x 4" rectangle, instead of drawn patterns. Fuse web to wrong side of the fabrics indicated for these pieces.)
3. Use scissors to cut out appliqué pieces along traced lines; use rotary cutting equipment to cut out appliqué pieces given as measurements. Remove paper backing from all pieces.

INVISIBLE APPLIQUÉ

This machine appliqué method uses clear nylon thread to secure the appliqué pieces. Transparent monofilament (clear nylon) thread is available in 2 colors: clear and smoke. Use clear on white or very light fabrics and smoke on darker colors.

1. Referring to diagram and/or photo, arrange prepared appliqués on the background fabric and follow manufacturer's instructions to fuse in place.
2. Pin a stabilizer, such as paper or any of the commercially available products, on wrong side of background fabric before stitching appliqués in place.
3. Thread sewing machine with transparent monofilament thread; use general-purpose thread that matches background fabric in bobbin.
4. Set sewing machine for a very narrow width (approximately $1/16$") zigzag stitch and a short stitch length. You may find that loosening the top tension slightly will yield a smoother stitch.
5. Begin by stitching 2 or 3 stitches in place (drop feed dogs or set stitch length at 0) to anchor thread. Most of the zigzag stitch should be done on the appliqué with the right edges of the stitch falling at the very outside edge of the appliqué. Stitch over all exposed raw edges of appliqué pieces.

6. (*Note:* Dots on **Figs. 23 - 28** indicate where to lea needle in fabric when pivoting.) For **outside corners**, stitch just past the corner, stopping with the needle in **background** fabric (**Fig. 23**). Raise presser foot. Pivot project, lower presser foot, an stitch adjacent side (**Fig. 24**).

Fig. 23

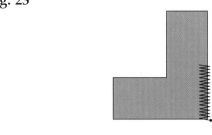

Fig. 24

7. For **inside corners**, stitch just past the corner, stopping with the needle in **appliqué** fabric (**Fig. 25**). Raise presser foot. Pivot project, lower presser foot, and stitch adjacent side (**Fig. 26**).

Fig. 25

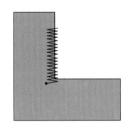

Fig. 26

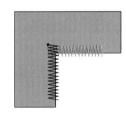

When stitching **outside** curves, stop with needle in **background** fabric. Raise presser foot and pivot project as needed. Lower presser foot and continue stitching, pivoting as often as necessary to follow curve (**Fig. 27**).

. 27

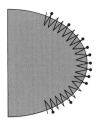

When stitching **inside** curves, stop with needle in **appliqué** fabric. Raise presser foot and pivot project as needed. Lower presser foot and continue stitching, pivoting as often as necessary to follow curve (**Fig. 28**).

. 28

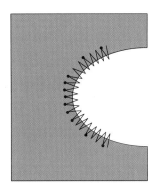

Do not backstitch at end of stitching. Pull threads to wrong side of background fabric; knot thread and trim ends.
Carefully tear away stabilizer.

AND APPLIQUÉ

*this traditional hand appliqué method, the needle is used
urn the seam allowance under as you sew the appliqué to
background fabric using a* **Blind Stitch***, page 127.*

Place template on right side of appliqué fabric. Use a pencil to lightly draw around template, leaving at least $1/2$" between shapes; repeat for number of shapes specified in project instructions.

2. Cut out shapes approximately $3/16$" outside drawn line. Clip inside curves and points up to, but not through, drawn line. Arrange shapes on background fabric and pin or baste in place.
3. Thread a sharps needle with a single strand of general purpose sewing thread; knot one end.
4. For each appliqué shape, begin on as straight an edge as possible and turn a small section of seam allowance to wrong side with needle, concealing drawn line. Use Blind Stitch to sew appliqué to background, turning under edge and stitching as you continue around shape. Do not turn under or stitch seam allowances that will be covered by other appliqué pieces.
5. Follow **Cutting Away Fabric From Behind Appliqués**, page 118, to reduce bulk behind appliqués.

MOCK HAND APPLIQUÉ

This technique uses the blindstitch on your sewing machine to achieve a look that closely resembles traditional hand appliqué. Using an updated method, appliqués are prepared with turned-under edges and then machine stitched to the background fabric. For best appliqué results, your sewing machine must have blindstitch capability with a variable stitch width. If your blindstitch width cannot be adjusted, you may still wish to try this technique to see if you are happy with the results. Some sewing machines have a narrower blindstitch width than others.

1. Follow project instructions to prepare appliqué pieces.
2. Thread needle of sewing machine with transparent monofilament thread; use general-purpose thread in bobbin in a color to match background fabric.
3. Set sewing machine for narrow blindstitch (just wide enough to catch 2 or 3 threads of the appliqué) and a very short stitch length (20 - 30 stitches per inch).
4. Arrange appliqué pieces on background fabric as described in project instructions. Use pins or hand baste to secure.

5. (*Note:* Follow Steps 6 - 9 of **Invisible Appliqué**, page 116, for needle position when pivoting.) Sew around edges of each appliqué so that the straight stitches fall on the background fabric very near the appliqué and the "hem" stitches barely catch the folded edge of the appliqué (**Fig. 29**)

Fig. 29

6. It is not necessary to backstitch at the beginning or end of stitching. End stitching by sewing $1/4$" over the first stitches. Trim thread ends close the fabric.

CUTTING AWAY FABRIC FROM BEHIND APPLIQUÉS

Hand quilting an appliquéd block will be easier if you are stitching through as few layers as possible. For this reason, or just to reduce bulk in your quilt, you may wish to cut away the background fabric behind appliqués. After stitching appliqués in place, turn block over and use sharp scissors or specially-designed appliqué scissors to trim away background fabric approximately $3/16$" from stitching line (**Fig 30**). Take care not to cut appliqué fabric or stitches.

Fig. 30

BORDERS

Borders cut along the lengthwise grain will lie flatter than borders cut along the crosswise grain. In most cases, our border lengths include an extra 2" at each end for bed-size quilts and an extra inch at each end for wall hangings for "insurance"; borders will be trimmed after measuring completed center section of quilt top.

ADDING SQUARED BORDERS

1. Mark the center of each edge of quilt top.
2. Squared borders are usually added to top and bottom, then side edges of the center section of a quilt top. To add top and bottom borders, measure across center of quilt top to determine length of borders (**Fig. 31**). Trim top and bottom borders to the determined length.
3. Mark center of 1 long edge of top border. Matching center marks and raw edges, pin border to quilt top, easing in any fullness; stitch. Repeat for bottom border.
4. Measure center of quilt top, including attached borders, to determine length of side borders. Trim side borders to the determined length. Repeat Step 3 to add borders to quilt top (**Fig. 32**).

Fig. 31

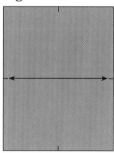

Fig. 32

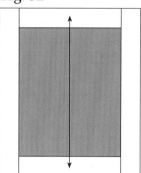

ADDING MITERED BORDERS

Mark the center of each edge of quilt top. Mark center of 1 long edge of top border. Measure across center of quilt top (see **Fig. 31**). Matching center marks and raw edges, pin border to center of quilt top edge. Beginning at center of border, measure $^1/_2$ the width of the quilt top in both directions and mark. Match marks on border with corners of quilt top and pin. Easing in any fullness, pin border to quilt top between center and corners. Sew border to quilt top, beginning and ending seams **exactly** $^1/_4$" from each corner of quilt top and backstitching at beginning and end of stitching (**Fig. 33**).

Fig. 33

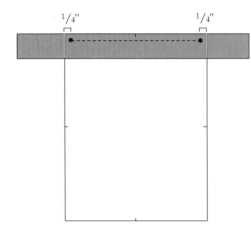

Repeat Step 2 to sew bottom, then side borders, to center section of quilt top. To temporarily move first 2 borders out of the way, fold and pin ends as shown in **Fig. 34**.

Fig. 34

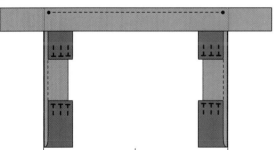

4. Fold 1 corner of quilt top diagonally with right sides together and matching edges. Use ruler to mark stitching line as shown in **Fig. 35**. Pin borders together along drawn line. Sew on drawn line, backstitching at beginning and end of stitching (**Fig. 36**).

Fig. 35

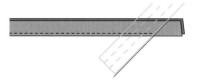

Fig. 36

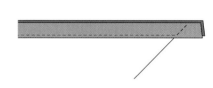

5. Turn mitered corner right side up. Check to make sure corner will lie flat with no gaps or puckers.
6. Trim seam allowance to $^1/_4$"; press to 1 side.
7. Repeat Steps 4 - 6 to miter each remaining corner.

QUILTING

Quilting holds the 3 layers (top, batting, and backing) of the quilt together and can be done by hand or machine. Our project instructions tell you which method is used on each project and show you quilting diagrams that can be used as suggestions for marking quilting designs. Because marking, layering, and quilting are interrelated and may be done in different orders depending on circumstances, please read the entire **Quilting** *section, pages 119 - 123, before beginning the quilting process on your project.*

TYPES OF QUILTING

In the Ditch

Quilting very close to a seamline (**Fig. 37**) or appliqué (**Fig. 38**) is called "in the ditch" quilting. This type of quilting does not need to be marked and is indicated on our quilting diagrams with blue lines close to seamlines. When quilting in the ditch, quilt on the side **opposite** the seam allowance.

Fig. 37

Fig. 38

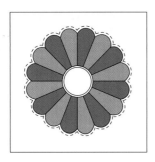

Outline Quilting

Quilting approximately $1/4$" from a seam or appliqué is called "outline" quilting (**Fig. 39**). This type of quilting is indicated on our quilting diagrams by blue lines a short distance from seamlines. Outline quilting may be marked, or you may place $1/4$"w masking tape along seamlines and quilt along the opposite edge of the tape. (Do not leave tape on quilt longer than necessary, since it may leave an adhesive residue.)

Fig. 39

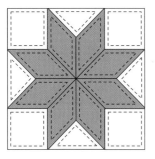

Ornamental Quilting

Quilting decorative lines or designs is called "ornamental" quilting (**Fig. 40**). Ornamental quilting indicated on our quilting diagrams by blue lines. This type of quilting should be marked before you baste quilt layers together.

Fig. 40

MARKING QUILTING LINES

Fabric marking pencils, various types of chalk markers, and fabric marking pens with inks that disappear with exposure to air or water are readily available and work well for different applications. Lead pencils work well on light-color fabrics, but marks may be difficult to remove. White pencils work well on dark-color fabrics, and silver pencils show up well on many colors. Since chalk rubs off easily, it's a good choice if you are marking as you quilt. Fabric marking pens make more durable and visible markings, but the marks should be carefully removed according to manufacturer's instructions. Press down only as hard as necessary to make a visible line.

When you choose to mark your quilt, whether before or after the layers are basted together, is also a factor deciding which marking tool to use. If you mark with chalk or a chalk pencil, handling the quilt during basting may rub off the markings. Intricate or ornamental designs may not be practical to mark as you quilt; mark these designs before basting using a more durable marker.

To choose marking tools, take all these factors into consideration and **test** different markers **on scrap fabric** until you find the one that gives the desired result.

USING QUILTING STENCILS

A wide variety of precut quilting stencils, as well as entire books of quilting patterns, are available. Using a stencil makes it easier to mark intricate or repetitive designs on your quilt top.

1. To make a stencil from a pattern, center template plastic over pattern and use a permanent marker to trace pattern onto plastic.
2. Use a craft knife with a single or double blade to cut narrow slits along traced lines (**Fig. 41**).

Fig. 41

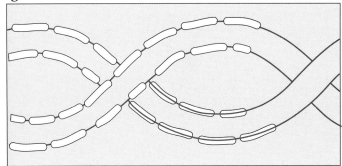

3. Use desired marking tool and stencil to mark quilting lines.

CHOOSING AND PREPARING THE BACKING

To allow for slight shifting of the quilt top during quilting, the backing should be approximately 4" larger on all sides for a bed-size quilt top or approximately 2" larger on all sides for a wall hanging. Yardage requirements listed for quilt backings are calculated for 45"w fabric. If you are making a bed-size quilt, using 90"w or 108"w fabric for the backing may eliminate piecing. To piece a backing using 45"w fabric, use the following instructions.

1. Measure length and width of quilt top; add 8" (4" for a wall hanging) to each measurement.
2. If quilt top is 76"w or less, cut backing fabric into 2 lengths slightly longer than the determined **length** measurement. Trim selvages. Place lengths with right sides facing and sew long edges together, forming a tube (**Fig. 42**). Match seams and press along 1 fold (**Fig. 43**). Cut along pressed fold to form a single piece (**Fig. 44**).

Fig. 42	Fig. 43	Fig. 44

 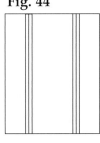

3. If quilt top is more than 76"w, cut backing fabric into 3 lengths slightly longer than the determined **width** measurement. Trim selvages. Sew long edges together to form a single piece.
4. Trim backing to correct size, if necessary, and press seam allowances open.

CHOOSING AND PREPARING THE BATTING

Choosing the right batting will make your quilting job easier. For fine hand quilting, choose a low-loft batting in any of the fiber types described here. Machine quilters will want to choose a low-loft batting that is all cotton or a cotton/polyester blend because the cotton helps "grip" the layers of the quilt. If the quilt is to be tied, a high-loft batting, sometimes called extra-loft or fat batting, is a good choice.

Batting is available in many different fibers. Bonded polyester batting is one of the most popular batting types. It is treated with a protective coating to stabilize the fibers and to reduce "bearding," a process in which batting fibers work their way out through the quilt fabrics. Other batting options include cotton/polyester batting, which combines the best of both polyester and cotton battings; all-cotton batting, which must be quilted more closely than polyester batting; and wool and silk battings, which are generally more expensive and usually only dry-cleanable.

Whichever batting you choose, read the manufacturer's instructions closely for any special notes on care or preparation. When you're ready to use your chosen batting in a project, cut batting the same size as the prepared backing.

ASSEMBLING THE QUILT

1. Examine wrong side of quilt top closely; trim any seam allowances and clip any threads that may show through the front of the quilt. Press quilt top.
2. If quilt top is to be marked before layering, mark quilting lines (see **Marking Quilting Lines**, page 120).
3. Place backing **wrong** side up on a flat surface. Use masking tape to tape edges of backing to surface. Place batting on top of backing fabric. Smooth batting gently, being careful not to stretch or tear. Center quilt top **right** side up on batting.

4. If hand quilting, begin in the center and work toward the outer edges to hand baste all layers together. Use long stitches and place basting lines approximately 4" apart (**Fig. 45**). Smooth fullness or wrinkles toward outer edges.

Fig. 45

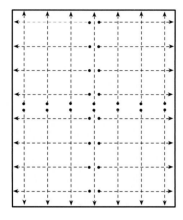

5. If machine quilting, use 1" rustproof safety pins to "pin-baste" all layers together, spacing pins approximately 4" apart. Begin at the center and work toward the outer edges to secure all layers. If possible, place pins away from areas that will be quilted, although pins may be removed as needed when quilting.

HAND QUILTING

The quilting stitch is a basic running stitch that forms a broken line on the quilt top and backing. Stitches on the quilt top and backing should be straight and equal in length.

1. Secure center of quilt in hoop or frame. Check quilt top and backing to make sure they are smooth. To help prevent puckers, always begin quilting in the center of the quilt and work toward the outside edges.
2. Thread needle with an 18" - 20" length of quilting thread; knot 1 end. Using a thimble, insert needle into quilt top and batting approximately $1/2$" from where you wish to begin quilting. Bring needle up at the point where you wish to begin (**Fig. 46**); when knot catches on quilt top, give thread a quick, short pull to "pop" knot through fabric into batting (**Fig. 47**).

Fig. 46   **Fig. 47**

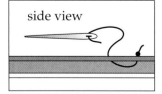

3. Holding the needle with your sewing hand and placing your other hand underneath the quilt, us thimble to push the tip of the needle down through all layers. As soon as needle touches yo finger underneath, use that finger to push the ti of the needle only back up through the layers to top of quilt. (The amount of the needle showing above the fabric determines the length of the quilting stitch.) Referring to **Fig. 48**, rock the needle up and down, taking 3 - 6 stitches before bringing the needle and thread completely through the layers. Check the back of the quilt to make sure stitches are going through all layers. When quilting through a seam allowance or quilting a curve or corner, you may need to mak 1 stitch at a time.

Fig. 48

4. When you reach the end of your thread, knot thread close to the fabric and "pop" knot into batting; clip thread close to fabric.
5. Stop and move your hoop as often as necessary. You do not have to tie a knot every time you move your hoop; you may leave the thread dangling and pick it up again when you return to that part of the quilt.

MACHINE QUILTING

The following instructions are for straight-line quilting, which requires a walking foot or even-feed foot. The term "straight-line" is somewhat deceptive, since curves (especially gentle ones) as well as straight lines can be stitched with this technique.

1. Wind your sewing machine bobbin with general-purpose thread that matches the quilt backing. Do not use quilting thread. Thread the needle of your machine with transparent monofilament thread if you want your quilting to blend with your quilt to fabrics. Use decorative thread, such as a metallic o contrasting-color general-purpose thread, when yc want the quilting lines to stand out more. Set the stitch length for 6 - 10 stitches per inch and attach the walking foot to sewing machine.

2. After pin-basting, decide which section of the quilt will have the longest continuous quilting line, oftentimes the area from center top to center bottom. Leaving the area exposed where you will place your first line of quilting, roll up each edge of the quilt to help reduce the bulk, keeping fabrics smooth. Smaller projects may not need to be rolled.

3. Start stitching at beginning of longest quilting line, using very short stitches for the first $1/4$" to "lock" beginning of quilting line. Stitch across project, using one hand on each side of the walking foot to slightly spread the fabric and to guide the fabric through the machine. Lock stitches at end of quilting line.

4. Continue machine quilting, stitching longer quilting lines first to stabilize the quilt before moving on to other areas.

BINDING

Binding encloses the raw edges of your quilt. Because of its stretchiness, bias binding works well for binding projects with curves or rounded corners and tends to lie smooth and flat in any given circumstance. It is also more durable than other types of binding. Binding may also be cut from the straight lengthwise or crosswise grain of the fabric. You will find that straight-grain binding works well for projects with straight edges.

MAKING CONTINUOUS BIAS STRIP BINDING

Bias strips for binding can simply be cut and pieced to the desired length. However, when a long length of binding is needed, the "continuous" method is quick and accurate.

1. Cut a square from binding fabric the size indicated in the project instructions. Cut square in half diagonally to make 2 triangles.

2. With right sides together and using a $1/4$" seam allowance, sew triangles together (**Fig. 49**); press seam allowance open.

Fig. 49

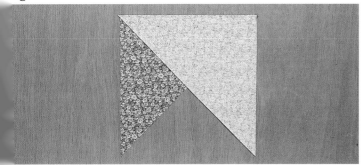

3. On wrong side of fabric, draw lines the width of the binding as specified in the project instructions, usually $2^{1}/2$" (**Fig. 50**). Cut off any remaining fabric less than this width.

Fig. 50

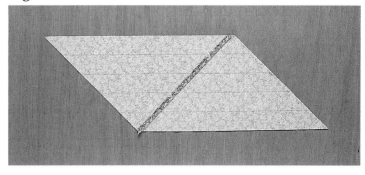

4. With right sides inside, bring short edges together to form a tube; match raw edges so that first drawn line of top section meets second drawn line of bottom section (**Fig. 51**).

Fig. 51

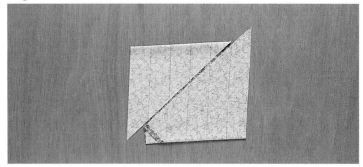

5. Carefully pin edges together by inserting pins through drawn lines at the point where drawn lines intersect, making sure the pins go through intersections on both sides. Using a $1/4$" seam allowance, sew edges together. Press seam allowance open.

6. To cut continuous strip, begin cutting along first drawn line (**Fig. 52**). Continue cutting along drawn line around tube.

Fig. 52

7. Trim ends of bias strip square.

8. Matching wrong sides and raw edges, press bias strip in half lengthwise to complete binding.

MAKING STRAIGHT-GRAIN BINDING

1. To determine length of strip needed if attaching binding with mitered corners, measure edges of the quilt and add 12".
2. To determine lengths of strips needed if attaching binding with overlapped corners, measure each edge of quilt; add 3" to each measurement.
3. Cut lengthwise or crosswise strips of binding fabric the determined length and the width called for in the project instructions. Strips may be pieced to achieve the necessary length.
4. Matching wrong sides and raw edges, press strip(s) in half lengthwise to complete binding.

ATTACHING BINDING WITH MITERED CORNERS

1. Press 1 end of binding diagonally (**Fig. 53**).

Fig. 53

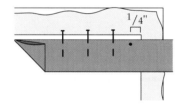

2. Beginning with pressed end several inches from a corner, lay binding around quilt to make sure that seams in binding will not end up at a corner. Adjust placement if necessary. Matching raw edges of binding to raw edge of quilt top, pin binding to right side of quilt along 1 edge.
3. When you reach the first corner, mark $1/4$" from corner of quilt top (**Fig. 54**).

Fig. 54

4. Using a $1/4$" seam allowance, sew binding to quilt, backstitching at beginning of stitching and when you reach the mark (**Fig. 55**). Lift needle out of fabric and clip thread.

Fig. 55

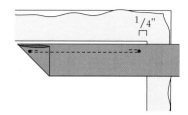

5. Fold binding as shown in **Figs. 56** and **57** and pin binding to adjacent side, matching raw edges. When you reach the next corner, mark $1/4$" from edge of quilt top.

Fig. 56

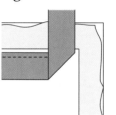

Fig. 57

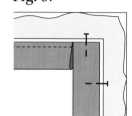

6. Backstitching at edge of quilt top, sew pinned binding to quilt (**Fig. 58**); backstitch when you reach the next mark. Lift needle out of fabric and clip thread.

Fig. 58

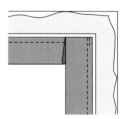

Repeat Steps 5 and 6 to continue sewing binding to quilt until binding overlaps beginning end by approximately 2". Trim excess binding.

If using 2¹/₂"w binding (finished size ¹/₂"), trim backing and batting a scant ¹/₄" larger than quilt top so that batting and backing will fill the binding when it is folded over to the quilt backing. If using narrower binding, trim backing and batting even with edges of quilt top.

On 1 edge of quilt, fold binding over to quilt backing and pin pressed edge in place, covering stitching line (**Fig. 59**). On adjacent side, fold binding over, forming a mitered corner (**Fig. 60**). Repeat to pin remainder of binding in place.

Fig. 59　　　　　**Fig. 60**

). Blindstitch binding to backing, taking care not to stitch through to front of quilt.

ATTACHING BINDING WITH OVERLAPPED CORNERS

Matching raw edges and using a ¹/₄" seam allowance, sew a length of binding to top and bottom edges on right side of quilt.

If using 2¹/₂"w binding (finished size ¹/₂"), trim backing and batting from top and bottom edges a scant ¹/₄" larger than quilt top so that batting and backing will fill the binding when it is folded over to the quilt backing. If using narrower binding, trim backing and batting even with edges of quilt top. Trim ends of top and bottom binding even with edges of quilt top. Fold binding over to quilt backing and pin pressed edges in place, covering stitching line (**Fig. 61**); blindstitch binding to backing.

Fig. 61

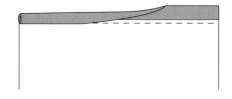

4. Leaving approximately 1¹/₂" of binding at each end, stitch a length of binding to each side edge of quilt. Trim backing and batting as in Step 2.
5. Trim each end of binding ¹/₂" longer than bound edge. Fold each end of binding over to quilt backing (**Fig. 62**); pin in place.

Fig. 62

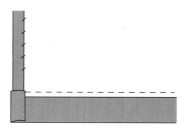

6. Fold binding over to quilt backing and blindstitch in place, taking care not to stitch through to front of quilt.

MAKING A HANGING SLEEVE

Attaching a hanging sleeve to the back of your wall hanging or quilt before the binding is added allows you to display your completed project on a wall.

1. Measure the width of the wall hanging top and subtract 1". Cut a piece of fabric 7"w by the determined measurement.
2. Press short edges of fabric piece ¹/₄" to wrong side; press edges ¹/₄" to wrong side again and machine stitch in place.
3. Matching wrong sides, fold piece in half lengthwise to form a tube.
4. Follow project instructions to sew binding to quilt top and to trim backing and batting. Before blindstitching binding to backing, match raw edges and stitch hanging sleeve to center top edge on back of wall hanging.
5. Finish binding wall hanging, treating the hanging sleeve as part of the backing.
6. Blindstitch bottom of hanging sleeve to backing, taking care not to stitch through to front of quilt.
7. Insert dowel or slat into hanging sleeve.

SIGNING AND DATING YOUR QUILT

Your completed quilt is a work of art and should be signed and dated. There are many different ways to do this, and you should pick a method that reflects the style of the quilt, the occasion for which it was made, and your own particular talents.

The following suggestions may give you an idea for recording the history of your quilt for future generations.

- Embroider your name, the date, and any additional information on the quilt top or backing. You may choose embroidery floss colors that closely match the fabric you are working on, such as white floss on a white border, or contrasting colors may be used.
- Make a label from muslin and use a permanent marker to write your information. Your label may be as plain or as fancy as you wish. Stitch the label to the back of the quilt.
- Chart a cross-stitch label design that includes the information you wish and stitch it in colors that complement the quilt. Stitch the finished label to the quilt backing.

PILLOW FINISHING

Any quilt block may be made into a pillow. If desired, you may add welting and/or a ruffle to the pillow top before sewing the pillow top and back together.

ADDING WELTING TO PILLOW TOP

1. To make welting, use bias strip indicated in project instructions. (Or measure edges of pillow top and add 4". Measure circumference of cord and add 2". Cut a bias strip of fabric the determined measurement, piecing if necessary.)
2. Lay cord along center of bias strip on wrong side of fabric; fold strip over cord. Using a zipper foot, machine baste along length of strip close to cord. Trim seam allowance to the width you will use to sew pillow top and back together (see Step 2 of **Making the Pillow**, page 127).

3. Matching raw edges and beginning and ending 3 from ends of welting, baste welting to right side pillow top. To make turning corners easier, clip seam allowance of welting at pillow top corners.
4. Remove approximately 3" of seam at 1 end of welting; fold fabric away from cord. Trim remaining end of welting so that cord ends meet exactly (**Fig. 63**).

Fig. 63

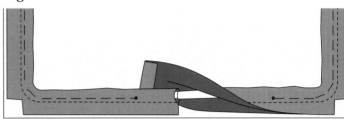

5. Fold short edge of welting fabric ¹/₂" to wrong side fold fabric back over area where ends meet (**Fig. 64**

Fig. 64

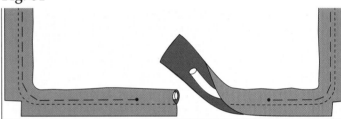

6. Baste remainder of welting to pillow top close to cord (**Fig. 65**).

Fig. 65

7. Follow **Making the Pillow** to complete pillow.

DDING RUFFLE TO PILLOW TOP

To make ruffle, use fabric strip indicated in project instructions.

Matching right sides, use a $1/4$" seam allowance to sew short edges of ruffle together to form a large circle; press seam allowance open. To form ruffle, fold along length with wrong sides together and raw edges matching; press.

To gather ruffle, place quilting thread $1/4$" from raw edge of ruffle. Using a medium-width zigzag stitch with medium stitch length, stitch over quilting thread, being careful not to catch quilting thread in stitching. Pull quilting thread, drawing up gathers to fit pillow top.

Matching raw edges, baste ruffle to right side of pillow top.

Follow **Making the Pillow** to complete pillow.

AKING THE PILLOW

For pillow back, cut a piece of fabric the same size as pieced and quilted pillow top.

Place pillow back and pillow top right sides together. The seam allowance width you use will depend on the construction of the pillow top. If the pillow top has borders on which the finished width of the border is not crucial, use a $1/2$" seam allowance for durability. If the pillow top is pieced so that a wider seam allowance would interfere with the design, use a $1/4$" seam allowance. Using the determined seam allowance (or stitching as close as possible to welting), sew pillow top and back together, leaving an opening at bottom edge for turning.

Turn pillow right side out, carefully pushing corners outward. Stuff with polyester fiberfill or pillow form and sew final closure by hand.

HAND STITCHES

Blind Stitch

Come up at 1. Go down at 2 and come up at 3 (**Fig. 66**). Length of stitches may be varied as desired.

Fig. 66

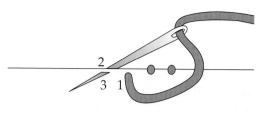

Satin Stitch

Come up at 1; go down at 2 and come up at 3. Continue until area is filled (**Fig. 67**).

Fig. 67

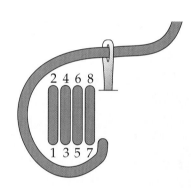

GLOSSARY

Appliqué — A cut-out fabric shape that is secured to a larger background. Also refers to the technique of securing the cut-out pieces.

Backing — The back or bottom layer of a quilt, sometimes called the "lining."

Backstitch — A reinforcing stitch taken at the beginning and end of a seam to secure stitches.

Basting — Large running stitches used to temporarily secure pieces or layers of fabric together. Basting is removed after permanent stitching.

Batting — The middle layer of a quilt that provides the insulation and warmth as well as the thickness.

Bias — The diagonal (45° for true bias) grain of fabric in relation to crosswise or lengthwise grain (see **Fig. 68**).

Binding — The fabric strip used to enclose the raw edges of the layered and quilted quilt. Also refers to the technique of finishing quilt edges in this way.

Blindstitch — A method of hand sewing an opening closed so that it is invisible.

Border — Strips of fabric that are used to frame a quilt top.

Chain piecing — A machine-piecing method consisting of joining pairs of pieces one after the other by feeding them through the sewing machine without cutting the thread between the pairs.

Grain — The direction of the threads in woven fabric. "Crosswise grain" refers to the threads running from selvage to selvage. "Lengthwise grain" refers to the threads running parallel to the selvages (**Fig. 68**).

Fig. 68

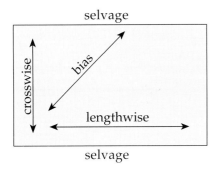

Machine baste — To baste using a sewing machine set at a long stitch length.

Miter — A method used to finish corners of quilt borders or bindings consisting of joining fabric pieces at a 45° angle.

Piecing — Sewing together the pieces of a quilt design to form a quilt block or an entire quilt top.

Pin basting — Using rustproof safety pins to secure the layers of a quilt together prior to machine quilting.

Quilt blocks — Pieced or appliquéd sections that are sewn together to form a quilt top.

Quilt top — The decorative part of a quilt that is layered on top of the batting and backing.

Quilting — The stitching that holds together the 3 quilt layers (top, batting, and backing); or, the entire process of making a quilt.

Sashing — Strips or blocks of fabric that separate individual blocks in a quilt top.

Seam allowance — The distance between the seam and the cut edge of the fabric. In quilting, the seam allowance is usually 1/4".

Selvages — The 2 finished lengthwise edges of fabric (see **Fig. 68**). Selvages should be trimmed from fabric before cutting.

Set (or Setting) — The arrangement of the quilt block as they are sewn together to form the quilt top.

Setting squares — Squares of plain (unpieced) fabric set between pieced or appliquéd quilt blocks in a quilt top.

Setting triangles — Triangles of fabric used around the outside of a diagonally set quilt top to fill in between outer squares and border or binding.

Stencil — A pattern used for marking quilting lines.

Straight grain — The crosswise or lengthwise grain of fabric (see **Fig. 68**). The lengthwise grain has the least amount of stretch.

Strip set — Two or more strips of fabric that are sewn together along the long edges and then cut apart across the width of the sewn strips to create smaller units.

Template — A pattern used for marking quilt pieces to be cut out.

Triangle-square — In piecing, 2 right triangles joined along their long sides to form a square with a diagonal seam (**Fig. 69**).

Fig. 69

Unit — A pieced section that is made as individual steps in the quilt construction process are completed. Units are usually combined to make blocks or other sections of the quilt top.